Building Security in Africa

An Evaluation of U.S. Security Sector Assistance in Africa from the Cold War to the Present

Stephen Watts, Trevor Johnston, Matthew Lane, Sean Mann, Michael J. McNerney, Andrew Brooks

Prepared for the Office of the Secretary of Defense
Approved for public release; distribution unlimited

For more information on this publication, visit www.rand.org/t/RR2447

Library of Congress Control Number: 2018953878
ISBN: 978-1-9774-0049-9

Published by the RAND Corporation, Santa Monica, Calif.

Cover: Photo by Staff Sgt. Brian Kimball.

Preface

This report documents the results of a RAND Corporation project, "The Effectiveness of Security Cooperation in Advancing Counterterrorism and Counterinsurgency Goals in Africa." The research team used statistical models to analyze the effects that U.S. security sector assistance (SSA) has on various forms of political violence (including civil wars and insurgencies, terrorism, and government repression) in the U.S. Africa Command area of responsibility.

The findings should interest those in the foreign policy and defense communities concerned about SSA and counterterrorism policies, especially in Africa but also more broadly. It should be of particular interest to policymakers and planners in the Office of the Secretary of Defense, U.S. Africa Command, the U.S. Department of State, and other stakeholders in the SSA process.

This research was sponsored by the Office of the Deputy Assistant Secretary of Defense for African Affairs in the Office of the Secretary of Defense and conducted within the International Security and Defense Policy Center of the RAND National Defense Research Institute, a federally funded research and development center sponsored by the Office of the Secretary of Defense, the Joint Staff, the Unified Combatant Commands, the Navy, the Marine Corps, the defense agencies, and the defense Intelligence Community.

For more information on the RAND International Security and Defense Policy Center, see www.rand.org/nsrd/ndri/centers/isdp or contact the director (contact information is provided on the webpage).

Contents

Figures and Tables

Figures

Tables

Summary

The Policy Debate over SSA in Africa

Both during the Cold War and in the post–Cold War period, the United States sought to combat security threats in Africa principally by supporting partner governments on the continent. Although the United States has maintained a small, enduring presence in Djibouti since the September 11, 2001, attacks, its direct military presence (or "footprint") has generally been quite small, consisting predominantly of trainers and advisers. It has only very rarely engaged in direct combat. The United States has remained consistent in this approach whether the perceived threat was communism, waves of refugees and potentially pandemic diseases spread in part by civil wars, or transnational terrorism. One of the primary instruments the United States uses to support its partners is *security sector assistance* (SSA), a term that encompasses transfers of military materiel, tactical combat training, joint exercises, military education for foreign military officers, defense institution building, and other types of security cooperation.

Proponents of SSA claim that it is a cost-effective tool for advancing U.S. interests on the continent while being acceptable to African partners of the United States. By strengthening partners' security capabilities, the United States can help partners deter challenges by militants and degrade and ultimately defeat those challenges that do arise. Moreover, by professionalizing and socializing partner security personnel, the United States can stabilize governments through improved civil–military relations and human-rights practices.

Critics, on the other hand, contend that SSA has undermined precisely the goals the United States is trying to achieve. By strengthening the military capabilities of African governments, the United States can unintentionally threaten ethnic groups that are excluded from government, in some cases causing them to take up arms to defend themselves. Because some communities in Africa do not trust the United States, even small amounts of SSA can sometimes spark rumors and mistrust, fueling the sorts of narratives through which terrorist groups recruit new followers. And providing additional capabilities to military forces can strengthen them relative to civilian government leaders and the public, potentially leading to coups or abuses of human rights.

Past Efforts to Evaluate SSA

Ideally, SSA allocations and practices would be guided by rigorous evaluations that would help to determine the conditions under which SSA is more or less effective. To date, nearly all evaluations of SSA's impact in Africa have been qualitative. Numerous case studies, after-action reports, lessons-learned exercises, and other efforts have yielded important insights. They have not, however, established a rigorous basis for determining overall trends. Even if SSA has had negative consequences in certain highly publicized cases, do we find positive net effects when we consider the large number of activities that never attract media attention? Conversely, even if we can point to success stories in the short term, are these successes sustained years after U.S. trainers depart? In some cases, such as the 2012 coup in Mali, proponents and opponents of SSA use different interpretations of the same incidents to make opposite arguments about how the United States should allocate SSA in the future. For all of the insights gained through qualitative analyses, there are limits to the guidance that they can provide for U.S. policy.

Quantitative analyses are more appropriate than qualitative ones for discerning overall trends. Unfortunately, such analyses require large amounts of relatively high-quality data, and such data are difficult to acquire for an analysis of the effects of SSA in Africa. Existing data sets provide fairly reliable information on many of the outcomes that the United States is trying to influence—for instance, the onset and duration of insurgencies, numbers of terrorist attacks and fatalities from those attacks, military coup attempts, and even overall assessments of African security forces' performance on international human-rights measures. Data on many of the contextual variables that would affect these outcomes are much more uneven. But surprisingly, obtaining data on U.S.-provided SSA is one of the greatest challenges. Important gaps in the data exist. Even where we can identify allocated funding, determining the country and year in which it was actually spent can be difficult. And even when we can overcome these challenges, record-keeping is typically driven by accounting rather than by analytic requirements, making it difficult to determine which types of SSA were being conducted where.

Perhaps because of these data issues, there have been relatively few efforts to quantitatively assess the overall impact of U.S.-provided SSA. Those studies that have attempted to do so have generally found little, if any, impact of SSA in Africa. SSA has generally been found to be most effective in more-developed countries and those with good governance, and many countries in Africa face challenges of both economic and political development.[1]

Goals and Research Approach for This Study

This report details the results of statistical analyses of the impact that U.S.-provided SSA has had in Africa. More specifically, the statistical

---

[1] See, for instance, Michael J. McNerney, Angela O'Mahony, Thomas S. Szayna, Derek Eaton, Caroline Baxter, Colin P. Clarke, Emma Cutrufello, Michael McGee, Heather Peterson, Leslie Adrienne Payne, and Calin Trenkov-Wermuth, *Assessing Security Cooperation as a Preventive Tool*, Santa Monica, Calif.: RAND Corporation, RR-350-A, 2014. That study found that U.S.-provided SSA generally yielded small but statistically significant gains in stability in U.S. partner nations but that this outcome was conditional on political and economic development. For those models that sought to isolate the effects of SSA in Africa, the authors found no statistically significant results.

models estimated the effects of SSA on the occurrence of three types of political violence on the continent:

- civil wars and insurgencies
- terrorism
- state repression.

These three outcomes do not exhaust the range of goals the United States attempts to secure through its SSA. The United States, for instance, seeks to gain access and influence with its partners. Thus, even if SSA fails to reduce violence, it might nonetheless succeed in the less ambitious goal of improving U.S. influence. On the other hand, the United States pursues goals even more ambitious than reducing violence. Ideally, SSA improves the overall quality of governance of partner states (e.g., by promoting democracy). By improving security and governance, SSA might also affect broader indicators of social well-being, such as life expectancy.

However, examining all possible effects of SSA in one study is impossible. Although the United States pursues multiple goals through its SSA, political violence is one key measure of impact. The 2015 U.S. Africa Command (AFRICOM) theater campaign plan, for instance, states that AFRICOM, "with partners, disrupts and neutralizes transnational threats, . . . prevents and mitigates conflict, and builds African partner defense capability and capacity in order to promote regional security."[2] Although the incidence of political violence is not the only criterion by which U.S. SSA should be judged, it clearly is one that is central to the expressed goals of such assistance.

We evaluated each of the three outcomes—civil wars and insurgencies, terrorism, and state repression—across all postindependence countries in Africa (except Egypt) after 1945 for which we had adequate data.[3] For each country, we determined (as precisely as the data

[2] Commander, AFRICOM, *Theater Campaign Plan 2000–16*, August 18, 2015, p. 15, not available to the general public.

[3] We excluded Egypt for two reasons. First, it lies outside the AFRICOM area of responsibility. For U.S. programmatic purposes, therefore, excluding it makes more sense. Second,

permitted) the amount of SSA (measured in constant dollars) the United States provided in each year. We could then compare levels of all three types of violence between countries that received significant SSA and those that received smaller amounts. Additionally, we could compare levels of violence over time within individual countries during years in which they received more or less assistance.[4]

The implications of this research extend well beyond Africa. Africa provides a useful regional focus for this analysis, however. First, it allows us to explore the effects of SSA in a region generally characterized by lower levels of development and higher fragility than the global average. Previous quantitative studies have found major differences in the effectiveness of SSA in more and less developed countries (e.g., Niger versus contemporary South Korea) but have found little variation in SSA's effectiveness between less developed countries.[5] Second, Africa (outside of Egypt) has generally been a lesser priority not only of the United States but also of other countries, such as Russia and China. We therefore do not have outliers, such as South Vietnam, post-2001 Afghanistan, or post-2003 Iraq, to skew our analysis.

We wrote the main body of this report using nontechnical language so that nonspecialists can understand our results, the modeling assumptions behind them, and their implications for U.S. policy. In Appendix B, we provide a detailed account of the dozens of models we ran to test alternative assumptions, alternative measures of our outcomes of interest, and alternative modeling strategies.[6] The results we report are generally robust across the wide range of tests that we posed for our initial findings.

Egypt receives large amounts of SSA, making it an extreme outlier in Africa. Including Egypt would skew our results for the rest of the continent.

4 We attempted to find alternative measures of SSA that would allow us to test more-precise relationships between different types or modalities of SSA and the outcomes of interest. As we describe in detail in Chapter Two, data-quality issues prevented us from undertaking these alternative approaches.

5 McNerney, O'Mahoney, et al., 2014.

6 The appendixes are available online on the product page for this report.

Although we used a variety of statistical techniques to mitigate the data challenges as much as possible, these issues nonetheless limited the levels of precision and nuance in our analysis. The findings that we report here represent broad trends. These trends are themselves an important advance on previous findings and, we hope, will open the way for future improvements in the evaluation of SSA. Because of these data and methodological challenges, however, this report is best understood as one step in a broader, multimethod evaluation agenda. As our findings suggest, there is considerable room to improve on U.S. SSA policies, and rigorous evaluations are a critical component of improving the design and implementation of those policies.

Research Findings on the Impact of SSA

The statistical analyses detailed in this report reveal broad trends with important implications both for policy and for future evaluations of SSA.

The United States Deemphasized Governance Issues During Cold War Competition

SSA appears to have been allocated very differently in the Cold War and post–Cold War periods. During the Cold War, the United States' primary goal was to maintain partnerships with governments in Africa and to prevent regimes from slipping into the Soviet orbit. Enhancing governance or human rights—or even maintaining peace and stability—was not the overriding goal of U.S. assistance in this period. Consistent with this reading of U.S. foreign policy is our finding that the United States was more likely to provide SSA to more-autocratic and more-corrupt governments in this period while unsurprisingly steering aid away from Soviet allies and partners. In the post–Cold War era, in contrast, the United States provided less aid to repressive governments. It also tended to prioritize countries recovering from civil wars. These findings are consistent with numerous studies that have found that U.S. development assistance was also targeted very differently in the Cold War and post–Cold War eras.

SSA in the Cold War Appears to Have Increased the Incidence of Civil Wars

The differences between the Cold War and post–Cold War eras are important from a policy perspective. Our statistical analyses found relatively few consistent relationships (positive or negative) between SSA and political violence across African countries. One of the exceptions was the relationship between SSA and civil wars during the Cold War: U.S. assistance appears likely to have increased the incidence of civil wars in this period.

There are at least two explanations for this relationship. First, because the United States emphasized international alignment over domestic stability as the primary goal of its assistance policies, it might have implemented SSA in ways that exacerbated conflict. As our first-stage models suggest, the United States was perfectly willing to collaborate with authoritarian and corrupt governments so long as they were not allies of the Soviet Union. Doing so might have prompted backlash among populations that were excluded from government. Second, at times, the Soviet Union countered U.S. assistance by providing aid to armed opposition movements, touching off proxy wars.

This finding is important not just for historical reasons. If international competition for influence in Africa again intensifies, the United States might again be tempted to deemphasize governance issues when it allocates SSA. Our analyses suggest that such an approach risks provoking higher levels of conflict on the continent.

Most SSA in Most Countries in the Post–Cold War Era Appears to Have Had Little Net Impact

We identified no robust statistical relationships between aggregate SSA and the incidence of political violence across all of Africa in the post–Cold War era. This absence of an overall relationship between U.S.-provided SSA and political violence does not necessarily mean that there is no effect. SSA might be having positive and negative effects in different countries at various times, depending on the context, in which case the divergent effects would result in no net impact. Similarly, if some U.S. programs had positive effects and others negative effects, there would be no net result. If the more-expensive forms of

SSA (such as equipment transfers) had no effect while very small-budget programs (such as International Military Education and Training) or recent programs (such as the Security Governance Initiative) had consistent effects, the much more-expensive programs might obscure the impact of the smaller programs.

Unfortunately, limitations in the data the United States has collected on its SSA expenditures prevented us from conducting program-specific evaluations. Some categories of SSA—especially relatively inexpensive ones and recent ones—might be successful. And some categories of SSA might be problematic. Until the U.S. government collects, stores, and disseminates more-precise data on SSA, conducting reliable statistical tests of more-nuanced and program-specific relationships will be extremely difficult.

Despite these data limitations, the lack of an aggregate effect of SSA is important. Whatever "success stories" might exist are relatively modest in their impact on political violence, obscured by much larger amounts of inefficient spending, or offset by counterproductive outcomes in other cases. Otherwise, our analyses should have detected some relationship between SSA and the incidence of political violence.

The finding that U.S.-provided SSA is not having any net impact on political violence in the post–Cold War era should not be altogether surprising. Previous analyses have found weaknesses in African partner nations' ability to sustain much of the equipment the United States provides and to disseminate the skills gained in U.S.-sponsored training events through train-the-trainer approaches. Whether because of maintenance problems, lack of training infrastructure, or other causes, the gains the United States' partners realize from SSA are often short-lived. Even if African partners could sustain these gains, those partners often appear to have difficulties harnessing these capabilities for effective political–military strategies. In some cases, U.S. partners might divert these capabilities to corrupt ends, while, in other cases, they might use them to try to repress nonstate actors where cooptation might be the more appropriate strategy.

The finding that U.S. assistance in the post–Cold War era has not had any identifiable net effect is an important one. It suggests, at a minimum, that U.S. efforts are often inefficient and wasteful. If U.S.-

provided SSA is indeed helping to build short-term, tactical capabilities but these capabilities are not sustained or attached to an effective political–military strategy, the United States needs to reallocate SSA to specific programs that it has strong reason to believe produce outcomes superior to the aggregate effects of SSA. If certain types of U.S. SSA are having divergent effects depending on context, the United States must employ risk analysis better to identify contexts in which SSA is having counterproductive effects.

SSA Has Had Significant, Positive Impact in Peacekeeping Contexts

Although SSA has not had any identifiable net effect on political violence across most countries on the continent, it *has* had a significant impact on the incidence of political violence when conducted in conjunction with United Nations (UN) peacekeeping operations (PKOs). Even when we control for the direct effects of "blue helmets," we find that SSA executed in the presence of peacekeepers has statistically significant, favorable effects on a range of outcomes. It decreases the likelihood of renewed conflict, terrorist attacks, and government repression.

A statistical analysis such as this one cannot uncover the precise reasons for these favorable effects. They are entirely consistent with the security sector reform (SSR) literature, however. The SSR paradigm emphasizes that the capabilities of security forces should be built in conjunction with improvements to security governance. The presence of a UN PKO typically provides many of the prerequisites for such an approach to succeed: regular, intensive contact between international advisers and the partner nation's security personnel; a relatively long-term commitment; close oversight of the performance of security forces; and integration of train-and-equip efforts into an overall political strategy. One of the criticisms of the SSR paradigm has been the relatively thin base of rigorous empirical support for its prescriptions. The statistical results presented in this report help to fill that gap and lend credence to the SSR school of thought.

Recommendations for the Allocation and Implementation of SSA

Our results have important implications for how the United States should allocate and implement SSA in the future.

Balance Goals of Achieving Access and Influence with Governance Concerns

In Africa, the United States' primary goals for SSA include building partner capacity to combat irregular threats (such as terrorism) and gaining access to and influence with important partner nations. The record of the Cold War suggests that these two goals can be at odds with one another. In attempting to ensure that partners in Africa remained aligned with the United States rather than the Soviet Union, the United States might well have aggravated domestic political tensions and ultimately increased the incidence of civil wars on the continent. Looking forward, many observers anticipate increased international competition for influence in Africa. China is the United States' primary concern, but other nations—including Russia, Turkey, and the Persian Gulf states—also play roles. The United States might again be tempted to relegate governance issues to second-tier status in an effort to maintain its existing partnerships. Doing so, however, could come at a sizable cost if it again enflames domestic political rivalries. The United States should balance its efforts to maintain influence in Africa with efforts to build partners' capabilities in a manner that avoids unintended adverse consequences.

Adopt a Comprehensive Approach with Persistent Presence and Oversight

The fact that U.S.-provided SSA had consistently positive effects in reducing violence when implemented in conjunction with UN PKOs suggests that the manner in which SSA is implemented is critical. Much of the SSA that the United States provides is highly episodic, built around particular targets of opportunity. In some cases, planners have had to expend so much effort to cobble together the necessary authorities, programs, and funding that they had insufficient time remaining to think about how individual SSA efforts fit into a comprehensive political–military approach. Moreover, legislative requirements and shifting senior-level attention often mean that efforts cannot be sustained over multiple years. The result is an inefficient expenditure of SSA funds, with many or most initiatives demonstrating little enduring impact. This is the conclusion that emerges from our statistical analysis, and it is the conclusion that many U.S. military personnel have reached through difficult personal experience.

The SSR paradigm suggests that tactical capability-building should be embedded within a comprehensive approach that is appropriate to the local political context, should involve close collaboration between foreign advisers and local stakeholders, and should be part of a long-term process. UN PKOs typically provide the organizational "scaffolding" for such an approach. Because the United States has interests in Africa outside of countries that are hosting PKOs, it needs a model of SSA that works outside of these most favorable contexts. A handful of U.S. programs—most notably, the Security Governance Initiative—adopt the principles of SSR but attempt to implement them in countries that are not hosting blue helmets. Unfortunately, these programs are of such recent origin that we could not test their effects in our models. The consistently favorable results of SSA in the context of PKOs and the absence of impact elsewhere, however, suggest that the United States should continue to find ways to implement these principles elsewhere when feasible.

Conduct Risk Assessments

Although U.S.-provided SSA is not having any net effect on levels of violence across all of the countries of Africa in the post–Cold War era, SSA might have divergent effects, depending on the type of SSA and the context in which it is implemented. The potential for counterproductive effects in certain contexts suggests that U.S. planners should undertake efforts to reduce political risk. If U.S. planners could successfully anticipate and at least partially mitigate the political risks of SSA through formal risk assessments at the outset of high-risk SSA programs, SSA might start to demonstrate a net positive effect on political violence. Although the statistical evidence of political risk is somewhat ambiguous, many qualitative analyses suggest factors to consider in assessing risk.

Recommendations for Future Assessment, Monitoring, and Evaluation

Although the broad trends identified in this report represent an important baseline for understanding the impact of SSA in Africa, much work remains to be done. Improving monitoring and data collection and dissemination for U.S. SSA is an important first step. There are also numerous opportunities to conduct much more-precise evaluations of SSA's impact in specific countries.

Commit to Rigorous Monitoring and Evaluation

The U.S. government has made considerable improvements in the past couple of years in its monitoring and evaluation policies for SSA in Africa and more generally. A robust monitoring and evaluation program can yield substantial returns on investment—but only if funding and effort are sustained over time. The U.S. government should continue its efforts to improve program monitoring, to systematize data collection and dissemination, and to use these inputs for improved evaluations.

Improve the Quality of SSA Data

Existing data on U.S.-provided SSA suffer from numerous problems of scope and quality that limit what SSA statistical evaluations are feasible. The U.S. government might undertake to improve data quality through several initiatives, ranging from improved accounting standards to improved guidance on how to write rigorous and useful after-action reports from security cooperation events. Improving data collection is only part of the challenge, however. For good data collection to truly be useful, the U.S. government must also commit to improved knowledge-management practices, including appropriate storage and dissemination.

Conduct In-Depth Evaluations of High-Impact, High-Risk Programs

As efforts to evaluate the effectiveness of development assistance have demonstrated, analyzing the impact of highly complex interventions in foreign countries is a challenging undertaking. No one form of evaluation can hope to grapple with this complexity. Up to this point, most evaluations of SSA have been qualitative. These analyses have provided many useful insights, but they are inherently limited in their ability to delineate broad trends. This study was perhaps the most in-depth quantitative analysis to date of SSA effectiveness in Africa. Although it has shed light on some critically important trends, it still represents only an initial effort.

Improved data collection would permit more-refined cross-national quantitative analyses, such as this one. But, ideally, such studies would be complemented by narrower, more-focused evaluations with much stronger methods for identifying the precise causal pathway linking foreign interventions (such as SSA) with the outcomes of interest. Such in-depth, rigorous evaluations could not be used widely, but they could be conducted for experimental or high-risk forms of SSA to help improve the overall state of understanding of the field.

Acknowledgments

We are grateful first and foremost to former Deputy Assistant Secretary of Defense for African Affairs Amanda J. Dory, who sponsored this research and oversaw its execution. Dory, along with Stephanie M. Burchard and Matthew Minatelli in her office, provided encouragement, support, and extremely helpful feedback throughout the study.

We also owe a debt to many people within and outside the U.S. government with whom we consulted on security sector assistance (SSA) programs, data and accounting practices related to these programs, and statistical models of SSA effectiveness. We can never fully acknowledge the insights we have gained both during this study and in prior research that helped to inform our work, but we would like to acknowledge a handful of people who were particularly helpful during this study. Jonathan Caverley at the Strategic and Operational Research Department of the Naval War College and Angela O'Mahony at RAND generously shared with us their time, insights, data, and replication files from their previous work on SSA. Evgeny Finkel at George Washington University and Dorothy Ohl (formerly at George Washington University) kindly shared with us data on coups that they had collected. At the State Department, several officers took the time to meet with us on multiple occasions to help us better understand the department's planning, programming, accounting, and evaluation practices. We also thank Natalie Ziegler for outstanding work to properly format this report and ensure its completeness.

Abbreviations

AFRICOM	U.S. Africa Command
AOR	area of responsibility
AU	African Union
BPC	building partner capacity
CAR	Central African Republic
CIRI	Cingranelli and Richards
CTFP	Combating Terrorism Fellowship Program
CTPF	Counterterrorism Partnerships Fund
DGP	data-generating process
DIB	defense institution building
DIRI	Defense Institutional Reform Initiative
DoD	U.S. Department of Defense
DRC	Democratic Republic of the Congo
DSCA	Defense Security Cooperation Agency
E-IMET	Expanded International Military Education and Training
FMF	foreign military financing

GDP	gross domestic product
GSCF	Global Security Contingency Fund
GTD	Global Terrorism Database
IMET	International Military Education and Training (program)
JCET	Joint Combined Exchange Training
M&E	monitoring and evaluation
MoDA	Ministry of Defense Advisors
n/a	not applicable
NDAA	National Defense Authorization Act
ODA	official development assistance
OECD	Organisation for Economic Co-operation and Development
OLS	ordinary least squares
O&M	operation and maintenance
PKO	peacekeeping operation
PME	professional military education
PREACT	Partnership for Regional East Africa Counterterrorism
PRIO	Peace Research Institute Oslo
SC	security cooperation
SGI	Security Governance Initiative
SOF	special operations forces
SSA	security sector assistance
SSR	security sector reform

TSCS	time-series cross-section
TSCTP	Trans-Sahara Counterterrorism Partnership
UCDP	Uppsala Conflict Data Program
UN	United Nations
UNAVEM	United Nations Angola Verification Mission
USAID	U.S. Agency for International Development

CHAPTER ONE

Introduction

Objectives of This Report

To achieve its security goals in Africa—above all, combating terrorism and insurgency—the United States prioritizes cooperation with African partner nations.[1] Rather than deploying large numbers of U.S. forces, as it has done in east Asia, Europe, and the Middle East, the United States has invested in building the security capabilities of its African partners. According to U.S. leaders, such investments have made both Africa and the United States more secure. For example, in the 2017 AFRICOM posture statement, AFRICOM commander Gen Thomas D. Waldhauser declared,

> Relatively small but wise investments in African security institutions today offer disproportionate benefits to Africa, Europe, and the United States in the future, creating mutual opportunities and reducing the risks of destabilization, radicalization, and per-

[1] The current U.S. Africa Command (AFRICOM) theater campaign plan, for instance, states, "Decisive efforts build capacity of and strengthen relationships with African partners. Decisive efforts represent the primary way that [AFRICOM] will be successful over time. Decisive efforts are executed through security force assistance (SFA) and exercises." Three of the five goals to be supported by these "decisive efforts" relate to terrorism and insurgency: neutralizing al-Shabaab (a jihadist fundamentalist group based in east Africa), degrading violent extremist organizations in the Sahel region (Africa between the desert and savannah regions in the west and north), and containing Boko Haram (another jihadist organization, based in northeastern Nigeria). The fifth focuses on building peacekeeping capacity (Commander, AFRICOM, *Theater Campaign Plan 2000–16*, August 18, 2015, not available to the general public).

> sistent conflict. . . . We must continue to enable African solutions by building partner capacity, instilling professionalism within defense forces, and increasing their respect for the rule of law.[2]

In contrast with this vision of the positive impact of U.S. security sector assistance (SSA) in Africa is critics' claim that such aid destabilizes the continent. Some suggest that U.S. military presence and SSA in Africa have fueled escalating terrorist violence.[3] Others claim that certain types of SSA lead to coups and government repression.[4]

Both proponents and opponents of such assistance in Africa have cited numerous examples to buttress their arguments—and, in many cases, both sides cite the same examples to make opposite points. Critics, for instance, point out that the leader of a successful coup in Mali, Captain Amadou Sanogo, had received extensive training through the U.S. International Military Education and Training (IMET) program. Such training might have given him skills and resources that aided in his coup attempt.[5] One of the U.S. special operations forces (SOF) officers who had spent considerable time in Mali, on the other hand, made the opposite argument. The problem with U.S. assistance to Mali, he argued, was not that it had provided too much but rather

---

[2] Thomas D. Waldhauser, *United States Africa Command 2017 Posture Statement*, statement before the U.S. Senate Committee on Armed Services, March 9, 2017b.

[3] See, for instance, Nick Turse, "Even AFRICOM's Own Commander Admits Its Strategy Is Not Working," *Nation*, August 2, 2016.

[4] A handful of quantitative studies have found broad relationships between U.S.-provided SSA and coups and repression globally. On coups, see, for instance, Jesse Dillon Savage and Jonathan D. Caverley, "When Human Capital Threatens the Capitol: Foreign Aid in the Form of Military Training and Coups," *Journal of Peace Research*, Vol. 54, No. 4, 2017, pp. 545–546. For a related argument about repression, see Sam R. Bell, K. Chad Clay, and Carla Martinez Machain, "The Effect of US Troop Deployments on Human Rights," *Journal of Conflict Resolution*, Vol. 61, No. 10, 2017, pp. 2020–2042. Some Africanists have made such charges with regard to specific countries in Africa. On the Kenya case, for example, see Beth Elise Whitaker, "Reluctant Partners: Fighting Terrorism and Promoting Democracy in Kenya," *International Studies Perspectives*, Vol. 9, No. 3, August 2008, pp. 254–271; and Jan Bachmann and Jana Hönke, "'Peace and Security' as Counterterrorism? The Political Effects of Liberal Interventions in Kenya," *African Affairs*, Vol. 109, No. 434, January 1, 2010, pp. 97–114.

[5] Savage and Caverley, 2017, pp. 545–546.

that it had not provided enough. Those Malian units that had engaged most frequently with U.S. forces actually fought against the units that launched the coup.[6]

This report uses statistical analyses to look beyond individual cases to assess broad trends in the relationship between U.S.-provided SSA and political violence in Africa. More specifically, it seeks answers to four sets of questions:

- What is the relationship between U.S.-provided SSA and the incidence of terrorism and civil wars? Can SSA be an effective tool for achieving U.S. counterterrorism and counterinsurgency goals?
- What is the relationship between U.S.-provided SSA and government repression? Are there trade-offs between U.S. efforts to disrupt, degrade, and ultimately defeat various militant organizations in Africa and the goal of developing partner security forces that operate according to the rule of law? Or are efforts to encourage respect for human rights broadly consistent with—and perhaps necessary for—efforts to defeat nonstate actors that pose a threat to the United States?
- Are certain types and modalities of U.S.-provided SSA more successful than others? Are some forms counterproductive?
- In what contexts is SSA most likely to achieve its goals? Are certain types of partner nations more-promising partners than others?

Reducing political violence is not the only goal the United States pursues through SSA. For instance, it seeks to gain access and influence with its partners through SSA. Thus, even if SSA fails to reduce violence, it might nonetheless be successful in the less ambitious goal of increasing U.S. influence. On the other hand, the United States pursues goals even more ambitious than reducing violence. Ideally, SSA improves the overall quality of governance of partner states (e.g., by promoting democracy). By improving security and governance, SSA

---

[6] Simon J. Powelson, *Enduring Engagement Yes, Episodic Engagement No: Lessons for SOF from Mali*, Monterey, Calif.: Naval Postgraduate School, master's thesis, December 2013.

might also affect broader indicators of social well-being, such as life expectancy.

It is impossible to examine all possible effects of SSA in one study, however. Although the United States pursues multiple goals through its SSA, focusing on levels of political violence as one key measure of impact is entirely reasonable. The 2015 AFRICOM theater campaign plan, for instance, stated that AFRICOM, "with partners, disrupts and neutralizes transnational threats, . . . prevents and mitigates conflict, and builds African partner defense capability and capacity in order to promote regional security."[7] Although the incidence of political violence is not the only criterion by which U.S. SSA should be judged, it clearly is one that is central to the expressed goals of such assistance.

Research Approach

To answer these questions, we conducted statistical analyses of all countries in Africa except Egypt, from 1946 (or the year of each country's independence) to 2014.[8] We assessed the relationship between U.S.-provided SSA to each country in Africa—both in aggregate and by certain types and modalities—and changes in the level of violence in those countries in subsequent years. To the best of our knowledge, the analyses described in this report provide the most-detailed statistical analyses to date of the relationship between U.S.-provided SSA and political violence in Africa, including terrorism, civil wars, and repression.

---

[7] Commander, 2015, p. 15.

[8] We excluded Egypt for two reasons. First, Egypt lies in the area of responsibility (AOR) of U.S. Central Command, not AFRICOM. Thus, excluding Egypt from our analyses makes the results more usable for the U.S. government. More fundamentally, the United States provides SSA for Egypt on a scale that dwarfs all other SSA in Africa—and indeed all other countries in the world, except for Israel and countries, such as Afghanistan and Iraq, in which the United States has been engaged in large-scale combat operations. As an extreme outlier, Egypt would obscure statistical relationships between SSA and violence in the rest of Africa.

The implications of this research extend well beyond Africa. Africa provides a useful regional focus for this analysis, however. First, it allows us to explore the effects of SSA in a region generally characterized by lower levels of development and higher fragility than the global average. Previous quantitative studies have found major differences in the effectiveness of SSA in more and less developed countries (e.g., Niger versus contemporary South Korea) but have found little variation in the SSA's effectiveness between less developed countries.[9] Second, Africa (outside of Egypt) has generally been a lesser priority not only of the United States but also of other countries, such as Russia and China. We therefore do not have outliers, such as South Vietnam, post-2001 Afghanistan, or post-2003 Iraq, to skew our analysis.

Broad statistical analyses such as the ones detailed here offer both advantages and disadvantages compared with the qualitative analyses that predominate in this field and with narrower statistical analyses of specific countries or programs. Broad, cross-national statistical analyses will never be as nuanced as qualitative case studies. And they lack the precision of quantitative analyses (such as randomized-control trials) of specific programs in specific countries. What qualitative or quantitative analyses of specific programs in specific contexts gain in nuance and precision, however, they lose in generalizability; we cannot be certain that the effects observed in one context will be applicable elsewhere, including in future cases about which policymakers must make decisions. Cross-national statistical analyses thus provide an important tool for understanding broad trends.[10]

---

[9] Michael J. McNerney, Angela O'Mahony, Thomas S. Szayna, Derek Eaton, Caroline Baxter, Colin P. Clarke, Emma Cutrufello, Michael McGee, Heather Peterson, Leslie Adrienne Payne, and Calin Trenkov-Wermuth, *Assessing Security Cooperation as a Preventive Tool*, Santa Monica, Calif.: RAND Corporation, RR-350-A, 2014.

[10] Qualitative analyses are generally best used for program evaluations and rapid learning. Experiments provide the strongest causal identification strategy, but they provide extremely narrow findings, applicable to one time and place but with highly uncertain generalizability to other conditions (in other words, they sacrifice external validity to maximize the internal validity of their findings). Quasi-experimental, observational studies, such as this one, suffer from inherent limitations to their internal validity; even when variables are included to "control" for the influence of contextual factors, it is impossible to be certain that identified

A full monitoring and evaluation (M&E) effort should therefore draw on multiple methods to develop as full a picture as possible of a given program or policy, using the strengths of one approach to offset the weaknesses of others. Many official evaluation manuals in the development community, which has spent decades using various evaluation techniques to improve the impact of its work, recommend multimethod approaches.[11] This report, therefore, does not aim to be definitive. Rather, it represents an important contribution to a broader evaluation effort.

Beyond the methodological challenges, an analysis such as this one must contend with issues of data quality. Ironically, the greatest data challenges we encountered did not pertain to Africa but to U.S. SSA expenditures. As we detail in Chapter Two, data on U.S.-provided SSA are not broken down in a way that permits us to disaggregate different types of SSA over extended periods. As a result, our analysis can assess only the aggregate effects of SSA; more-nuanced assessments of certain types of SSA were not possible with the data available. Our results thus disproportionately reflect the effects of "big-ticket" (expensive forms of) SSA. Smaller, more-targeted programs might well have effects that were not distinguishable with the data available. The analysis detailed in this report is nonetheless valuable to understand the overall impact of U.S.-provided SSA. At a minimum, we hope, it will help to spur future efforts to improve data collection on SSA (as

---

relationships are causal rather than representing mere correlation. On the other hand, they have inherent advantages in establishing broadly generalizable patterns.

[11] See, for instance, U.S. Agency for International Development (USAID), *Assessing and Learning: ADS Chapter 203*, Washington, D.C., partial revision, February 10, 2012; and Mari Clark, Rolf Sartorius, and Michael Bamberger, *Monitoring and Evaluation: Some Tools, Methods and Approaches*, Washington, D.C.: World Bank, working paper, January 9, 2004. See also Dani Rodrik, "The New Development Economics: We Shall Experiment, but How Shall We Learn?" in Jessica Cohen and William Easterly, eds., *What Works in Development? Thinking Big and Thinking Small*, Washington, D.C.: Brookings Institution Press, November 3, 2009, pp. 24–47.

mandated in recent legislation) to enable testing of whether individual SSA programs do indeed result in different outcomes.[12]

Organization of This Report

The main body of this report presents the results of our analysis in nontechnical terms understandable to an audience without a background in statistics. For those readers interested in the details of the analyses, we describe all of the models and data in depth in a series of appendixes, all of which are available online at the product page for this report.[13] Chapter Two provides background on SSA, including definitions, types of SSA, descriptive statistics on where it has been allocated over time in Africa, and a brief discussion of the data challenges involved in evaluating SSA. Chapter Three provides an overview of the debates surrounding SSA in Africa. Many of the countries in Africa are fragile states characterized by tense interethnic relations, poor records of respect for human rights, and weak traditions of civilian control over the military. In such contexts, the injection of military assistance can potentially prove destabilizing. That chapter summarizes the arguments of those who believe that U.S. assistance can help to stabilize these countries by professionalizing their militaries and those who believe that U.S. assistance further exacerbates the underlying sources of fragility. It then formalizes these arguments into testable propositions. Chapter Four sets out our statistical research design. Chapter Five summarizes the findings of our research: It describes the statistical evidence for the consequences that U.S.-provided SSA has for the occurrence of civil wars, terrorism, and state repression. Chapter Six offers recommendations, both for U.S. policies on SSA and future

---

[12] Said legislation is the National Defense Authorization Act (NDAA) for Fiscal Year 2017 (Pub. L. 114-328, December 23, 2016).

[13] In Appendix C, we also conduct a related but distinct analysis on SSA's effects on coup propensity. Although it is an important topic and one that has recently received significant attention in some policymaking circles, the study of coups introduces a few particular challenges and requires a different strategy for measuring SSA. As such, we leave this analysis to that appendix and encourage interested readers to refer to it for a deeper discussion.

efforts to evaluate SSA. Appendix A summarizes the SSA programs we reviewed; Appendix B details the model and other technical material, and Appendix C discusses coups in further detail.

CHAPTER TWO

U.S. SSA in Africa

Before reviewing arguments about the effectiveness of SSA and explaining our approach to evaluating its effects, we must explain exactly what SSA is and how it has been allocated over time. This chapter first provides an overview of SSA, including definitions, purposes, and programs. It then provides descriptive statistics on where SSA is implemented and how patterns in U.S.-provided SSA have changed over time. Finally, the chapter briefly discusses some of the challenges associated with SSA data.

What Is SSA?

SSA is an official term that refers to all U.S. material and programmatic efforts to influence, engage, and support partner-state security institutions. *SSA* encompasses all related terms, such as *security force assistance*, *security cooperation* (SC), *building partner capacity* (BPC), *security sector reform* (SSR), *defense institution building* (DIB), and *foreign internal defense*. SSA includes engagement with all types of partner security sector actors, including the military, police, and judiciary, as well as related government and civil society stakeholders.[1]

The vast majority of U.S.-provided SSA falls under the authority of the U.S. Department of Defense (DoD) (as established in Title 10 of

[1] This definition of *SSA* is from Presidential Policy Directive 23 (White House, Office of the Press Secretary, "Fact Sheet: U.S. Security Sector Assistance Policy," Presidential Policy Directive 23, April 5, 2013).

the U.S. Code) and the State Department (as established in Title 22).[2] The Departments of Energy, Justice, Treasury, and Homeland Security also share a responsibility and support SSA, but to a much lesser degree than DoD and State.[3] DoD has long been involved in the planning and execution of many State Department SSA programs, particularly those, such as Foreign Military Financing (FMF), that involve partner-nation militaries. DoD tends to have less direct involvement in SSA programs assisting partner-nation police and other nonmilitary security actors, however. Historically, State Department SSA funds have generally exceeded those of DoD, although, in recent years, DoD levels have overtaken those of the State Department.[4]

In Africa, the U.S. military relies on SSA as the "decisive effort of [its] strategy," given "limited available resources, both financial and personnel, to accomplish U.S. objectives" in the region otherwise.[5] Foremost among these objectives are countering terrorism and violent extremist organizations, maintaining internal peace, and supporting

---

[2] U.S. Code, Title 10, Armed Forces, Subtitle A, General Military Law, Part IV, Service, Supply, and Procurement, Chapter 136, Provisions Relating to Specific Programs, Section 2282, Authority to Build the Capacity of Foreign Security Forces. The National Guard's State Partnership Program (as established in U.S. Code, Title 32, National Guard) is also under the authority of DoD. Other U.S. agencies, including the Departments of Energy, Justice, Treasury, and Homeland Security, are also involved in the provision of specific types of SSA. However, these programs tend to be relatively small, are often authorized and funded under interagency agreements with either DoD or the State Department (as in the U.S. Department of Justice's International Criminal Investigative Training Assistance Program), and might provide little publicly available information (as with any SSA administered by the Central Intelligence Agency).

[3] Nina M. Serafino, *Security Assistance and Cooperation: Shared Responsibility of the Departments of State and Defense*, Washington, D.C.: Congressional Research Service, R44444, April 4, 2016, p. 3.

[4] Rose Jackson, *Untangling the Web: A Blueprint for Reforming American Security Sector Assistance*, Washington, D.C.: Open Society Foundations, January 2017, p. 11. In Africa, the increase in DoD's relative share of SSA funding is in part due to the creation of the Counterterrorism Partnerships Fund (CTPF) in 2014, most of which goes to DoD's Section 2282 (formerly 1206) SSA program.

[5] Thomas D. Waldhauser, *General Thomas D. Waldhauser, Commander, U.S. Africa Command: Prepared Opening Statement, U.S. Senate Armed Services Committee, March 9, 2017*, statement before the U.S. Senate Committee on Armed Services, March 9, 2017a, p. 5.

regional peacekeeping operations (PKOs).[6] SSA in support of these goals takes many forms. The vast majority of outlays and programs provides equipment and training intended to build partner forces' tactical capacity (both actual combat capabilities and a variety of tactical-level support functions). Much smaller programs provide professional military education (PME) and advisory support to national-level security institutions. (In Appendix A, we summarize the various types of SSAs.)

Much of U.S. SSA is focused on BPC at the tactical level in support of forces conducting counterterrorism, counterinsurgency, and PKOs.[7] Partner security forces are outfitted with equipment and materiel, ranging from rifles to vehicle components to aircraft, under DoD's Section 2282 (global counterterrorism train-and-equip) program, the State Department's FMF and PKO accounts, and other SSA programs.[8] Many U.S. military engagements in Africa, whether Joint Combined Exchange Training (JCET) events or the annual Flintlock exercise in northwest Africa, are also focused on building partners' tactical capabilities, including the effective use of U.S.-provided equipment. The United States also sometimes provides instruction on small-unit leadership, equipment maintenance, and other tactical capabilities through IMET and the Combating Terrorism Fellowship Program (CTFP), which sponsor foreign military personnel's attendance at U.S. military schools and courses.

Some U.S. SSA focuses on building partner forces' capacity in higher-level functions, such as logistics, intelligence, personnel management, and operational planning. This is particularly true of SSA delivered in the form of PME under IMET and CTFP, although U.S.

---

6 Waldhauser, 2017a.

7 The distinctions between counterterrorism, counterinsurgency, and PKOs are sometimes blurred, particularly in the areas of Africa that are of greatest priority to the United States. In both Somalia and Mali, for example, peacekeeping missions include supporting host-nation forces against armed groups engaged in insurgency or terrorism.

8 Section 2282 (formerly Section 1206) and several other DoD programs were consolidated and reorganized by the NDAA for Fiscal Year 2017 (Pub. L. 114-328, 2016). Because this report evaluates the effects of U.S. SSA from 1945 to 2015, it refers to these programs using their historical rather than post-2016 labels.

exercises and training engagements in Africa sometimes include capacity building in these functions as well. At times, the United States also provides advisory support in these areas directly to partner-nation defense officials, often at the ministerial level. The Defense Institutional Reform Initiative (DIRI) is the prime example of this type of effort.[9]

In some cases, U.S. SSA supports security sector governance and capacity building at the institutional and strategic levels. This is often referred to as *DIB* and is a main emphasis of DoD's DIRI and Ministry of Defense Advisors (MoDA) programs. This type of SSA focuses on building partners' capacity to engage in such functions as strategic planning, doctrine development, resource management, and oversight. As part of this, U.S. DIB efforts often include a focus on strengthening partner–security force accountability. Examples of this type of DIB include the State Department's support to Kenya's Independent Policing Oversight Authority or the Defense Institute of International Legal Studies' efforts to strengthen the Democratic Republic of the Congo's (DRC's) military justice system. These accountability-focused efforts at the institutional level are often complemented by the inclusion of human-rights, civilian-control-of-the-military, and rule-of-law topics in U.S. training programs that build partner capacity at the unit or individual level, such as IMET. Although these programs provide critical support to defense institutions that are often extremely weak among African partner nations, they account for less than 5 percent of all U.S.-provided SSA.[10]

In practice, U.S. SSA to a particular partner often takes multiple forms and can focus on support at both the tactical and strategic levels. In the farthest-reaching efforts, the United States assists partner security institutions in all functions concurrently, from organizing the ministry of defense to establishing logistics networks to provid-

---

[9] Michael J. McNerney, Stuart E. Johnson, Stephanie Pezard, David Stebbins, Renanah Miles, Angela O'Mahony, Chaoling Feng, and Tim Oliver, *Defense Institution Building in Africa: An Assessment*, Santa Monica, Calif.: RAND Corporation, RR-1232-OSD, 2016, pp. 34–35.

[10] A recent RAND study found that no more than 5 percent of AFRICOM SSA funds were spent on DIB in 2013 and 2014 (McNerney, Johnson, et al., 2016, pp. 28–29).

ing ground troops with marksmanship training, as was undertaken in Liberia after the end of its civil war in 2003.[11]

Where and How Is SSA Delivered?

To understand the effects of SSA, we must first have a sense of the scale of U.S.-provided SSA and how it has changed over time. Figure 2.1 plots total SSA from 1946 to 2014, with separate trend lines for Africa, Asia, the Middle East, and South America. As discussed in greater detail later in this chapter, SSA is measured here as obligations in constant 2014 U.S. dollars and includes a variety of spending accounts found in the USAID Greenbook.[12] Among these regions, Asia and the Middle East have regularly seen the largest volume of SSA over time. But even these regions have experienced dramatic variation. SSA to Asia reached its highest levels in the early 1970s, representing U.S. support during the Vietnam War. After decades of relatively small amounts, SSA to Asia again picked up in the mid-2000s with the U.S. intervention in Afghanistan. The Middle East has seen similarly large changes, with SSA growing dramatically after the 1979 Camp David Accords, which provided more than $14 billion to Israel and Egypt.[13] SSA to the Middle East was largely stable through the 1980s and 1990s, increasing again in the mid-2000s with the U.S. intervention in Iraq. Compared with these regions, however, South America and Africa have received very little SSA. Both regions have seen periodic spikes in SSA but have

[11] Sean McFate, *Building Better Armies: An Insider's Account of Liberia*, Carlisle Barracks, Pa.: U.S. Army War College, Strategic Studies Institute, November 2013.

[12] All data on SSA are taken from the USAID Greenbook (USAID, *U.S. Overseas Loans and Grants: Obligations and Loan Authorizations, July 1, 1945–September 30, 2016*, CONG-R-0105, c. 2016). See the following section for a discussion of the limitations on Greenbook data. To create our aggregate SSA measure for these figures and the later analysis, we combined funds from the following accounts: Narcotics Control; Nonproliferation, Anti-Terrorism, Demining and Related; Cooperative Threat Reduction Account, Defense; Drug Interdiction and Counter-Drug Activities, Defense; FMF Program; IMET; Other Military Assistance; and PKOs.

[13] Framework for Peace in the Middle East and Framework for the Conclusion of a Peace Treaty Between Egypt and Israel, Israel–Egypt–United States, September 17, 1978.

Figure 2.1
Regional Trends in Provision of SSA

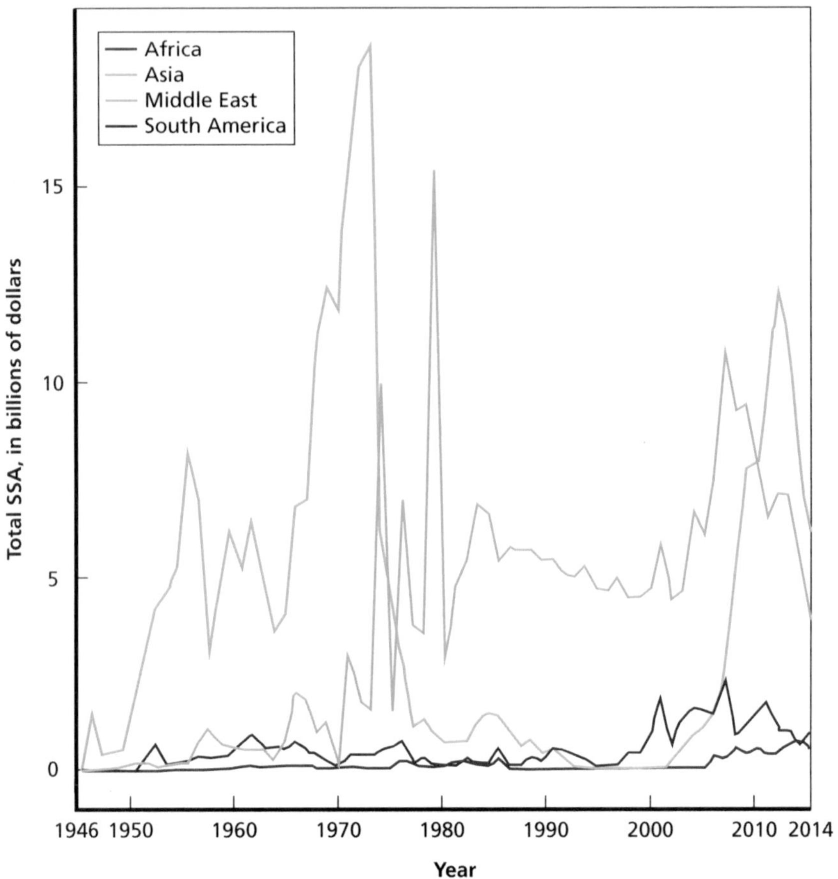

NOTE: All data on SSA come from the USAID Greenbook (USAID, 2016).
RAND *RR2447-2.1*

traditionally received much less assistance, albeit with a notable rise since the end of the 1990s.

To help the reader better visualize these changes for Africa, Figure 2.2 plots total SSA to countries in the AFRICOM AOR. On this smaller scale, we can more easily see the significant change in SSA to Africa over time. During the Cold War, annual changes in SSA

Figure 2.2
Historical Trends in SSA to Countries in the U.S. Africa Command Area of Responsibility

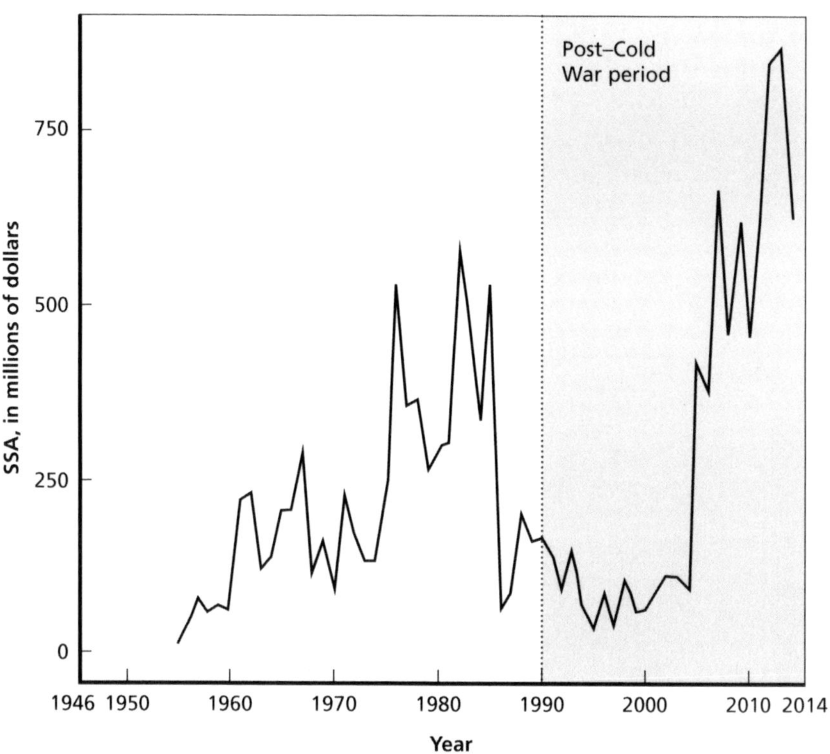

RAND *RR2447-2.2*

could be stark, with increases as large $280 million (1975–1976) and reductions of as much as $460 million (1985–1986). Such variation might reflect policy change from year to year, programmatic cycles, or even varying accounting practices.

More generally, though, we see that the post–Cold War period, represented by the shaded area to the right of the red dashed line, is somewhat more stable, albeit broken into two distinct subperiods. The early years (e.g., 1991 to 2004) were characterized by low levels of SSA, ranging from a relative high of $144 million in 1993 to a low of $36 million in 1995. Beginning in 2005, however, SSA dramatically increased in Africa. SSA has not dropped below $415 million since 2006 and reached a high of $868 million in 2013. These latter years coincide with the Global War on Terrorism, when the United States increased its attention on building partner-nation capabilities to combat terror and ensure regional stability. Overall, Figure 2.2 offers clear evidence that SSA allocation, at least in terms of aggregate assistance, changed significantly from the Cold War to post–Cold War periods.

Such change can also be seen in the share of African countries receiving aid, as depicted in Figure 2.3. In addition to aggregate spending, the number of SSA recipients has also increased over time, with the largest change actually coming in the 1980s. Although the early

Figure 2.3
Recipients of SSA in the U.S. Africa Command Area of Responsibility

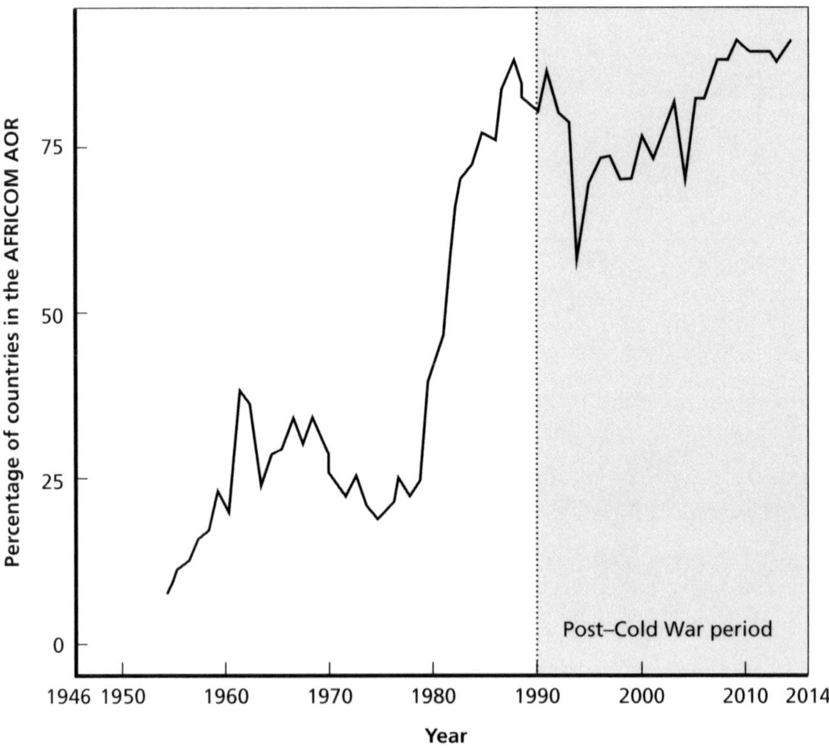

RAND *RR2447-2.3*

1960s saw a relatively large, sharp increase in the percentage of countries receiving aid (e.g., an 18-point change from 1961 to 1962), this growth is much smaller than the sustained increase of the 1980s (e.g., a 45-point change from 1980 to 1987). Until 1982, the majority of African states did not receive any SSA in a given year. But, since 1981, the number of SSA recipients has increased significantly and remained fairly stable, around 90 percent, from 2009 to 2014.

Overall, we see that the post–Cold War period has generally been associated with more SSA in Africa and a greater number of overall recipients. It is important to keep in mind, however, that most African partner nations receive only a small amount of assistance in any given year, often in the form of IMET for a relatively small number of military personnel. Long-standing priority partners (such as Kenya, Morocco, and Uganda) receive more assistance, and, among the poorer countries of Africa, even small absolute amounts of SSA can represent a major source of assistance. For example, Burundi, Djibouti, Niger, and Uganda each received U.S. SSA worth more than 15 percent of its military budget in 2012.[14] Even these larger efforts, however, tend to be concentrated in a few areas, such as provision of U.S.-made equipment, training for specific counterterrorism or peacekeeping units, or strengthening border security.

How Does the United States Monitor SSA?

U.S. assistance is splintered among a wide array of programs, each with its own goals, procedures, and accounting practices. This complexity greatly complicates efforts to monitor and evaluate SSA.

The USAID Greenbook represents the authoritative data set on all forms of U.S. foreign assistance and serves as our main source for SSA data.[15] Although the Greenbook aggregates data from dozens of U.S.

---

[14] Data on U.S. military assistance come from the USAID Greenbook (USAID, 2016). Data on African states' military budgets come from International Institute for Strategic Studies, *The Military Balance*, Vol. 114, No. 1, 2014.

[15] USAID, 2016.

government agencies and offices, all SSA funds since 1946 to countries in the AFRICOM AOR were managed by either DoD or the State Department, which report annual obligations and loan authorizations. USAID manages these records over time and uses an inflation adjustment to standardize historical data in terms of constant dollars. Most funds are recorded at the country-year-program level; for instance, the Greenbook indicates that Ethiopia received $1.7 million from IMET in 1955.

Unfortunately, accounting practices are not consistent across all SSA programs or accounts. Even where they are consistent, accounting practices are often driven by legal compliance requirements, without any attention to the types of data required for systematic evaluation of SSA's effectiveness. More specifically, we find, U.S.-compiled SSA data suffer from five shortcomings.

- First, Greenbook data sometimes fail to assign SSA expenditures to the appropriate country. The PKO account, for instance, typically assigns SSA expenditures to the country that is hosting a PKO. But much of the actual funds might be spent on other countries' militaries. PKO funds that are recorded as being spent on Somalia, for instance, might, in fact, be spent in the countries that are contributing troops to the African Union Mission in Somalia. It is thus impossible to determine, based on these data, what proportion of these funds has been spent where.
- Second, the Greenbook does not consistently assign funds to the appropriate year. There is a lag between when SSA funds are allocated and when they are executed—a lag that typically is no more than a year but can potentially last years for multiyear programs. The staff assigned to compile data for the Greenbook attempts to record SSA funds for the year in which they were executed. But incomplete and inconsistent data-gathering sometimes results in SSA being assigned to the wrong year in the Greenbook database. Although some errors might be corrected in future updates to the data, this procedure does not appear to be consistent across all reporting units, limiting USAID's ability to resolve all data problems. Such inconsistencies pose some challenges to any analysis,

such as ours, that attempts to measure changes in outcomes relative to changes in SSA on a year-by-year basis.

- Third, Greenbook data are organized by program. USAID's definition of *program*, however, does not always correspond to how others think about SSA programs and spending. In some cases, such as IMET, the designation perfectly maps onto a specific SSA program. For IMET and similarly mapped programs, we can precisely track the spending for each country over time. In other cases, however, the program includes a variety of distinct and nested accounts, often with unrelated purposes. For example, consider the account category Other Military Assistance. This account includes a variety of subaccounts, such as Operation and Maintenance (O&M), which can be further disaggregated. Within O&M, we find important SSA programs, such as Section 2282 (formerly Section 1206), that further combine materiel transfers with training and education. It is impossible, however, to determine which proportion of a given program's funds were used for which types of activities. This lack of transparency makes it impossible to evaluate the differential effectiveness of various types of SSA. In addition, data on certain programs, such as Section 1208 of the NDAA for Fiscal Year 2005, which provides SSA to partner forces working with U.S. SOF, are classified and thus not publicly available.[16]
- Fourth, Greenbook data ultimately account only for aid transferred to U.S. partners. They do not account for any activity that is conducted primarily for the benefit of U.S. forces. In an exercise such as Operation Flintlock in Africa, for instance, Greenbook data might account for much of the assistance provided to U.S. partners to facilitate their participation (such as funds to defray the costs of their fuel requirements). They would not, however, account for the U.S. SOF who participate in that exercise, despite

[16] Pub. L. 108-375, Ronald W. Reagan National Defense Authorization Act for Fiscal Year 2005, October 28, 2004; Lauren Ploch Blanchard, *Statement of Lauren Ploch Blanchard, Specialist in African Affairs, Congressional Research Service, Before the Senate Foreign Relations Committee Subcommittee on Africa and Global Health, Hearing: U.S. Security Assistance in Africa*, Washington, D.C.: Congressional Research Service, June 4, 2015, p. 12.

the fact that these forces provide valuable training to their partners, because the participation of U.S. SOF is considered primarily a training activity for the U.S. forces themselves. Similarly, JCET events are not accounted for as part of U.S. SSA expenditures; because their primary goal is to train U.S. SOF (to improve their ability to train foreign forces), their benefits to partner units are considered "incidental."[17]

- Finally, Greenbook data do not account for many of the subtleties of program execution. For instance, did equipment provided to U.S. partners arrive in time for a training event to take place as scheduled? If not, the funds spent on that training event might have been largely wasted. In such cases, it is difficult to determine whether this category of training is itself ineffective or whether it is ineffective only when improperly executed.

Many in the SSA community recognize these shortcomings, and many stakeholders have been undertaking efforts to improve their M&E practices. The State Department's Bureau of African Affairs and Bureau of Political–Military Affairs, for instance, have recently initiated some highly promising M&E efforts. Because of the recency of such initiatives, however, they will not allow for impact-level evaluations for many years to come—and even then, only if they receive the sustained funding and support necessary to gather data consistently over several years.

Despite these challenges, it is possible to use existing SSA data to conduct certain types of impact evaluations. But the data limitations inevitably limit the nuance of the analyses that can be undertaken and the likelihood of identifying robustly statistically significant results. Chapter Three summarizes ongoing debates about the effectiveness of SSA. Chapter Four explains which of those debates can be addressed with the data available and describes the procedures we used to mitigate the challenges that existing sources of data pose. Our analysis was able to identify some broad trends with important implications

[17] Defense Security Cooperation Agency (DSCA), "SAMM Chapters," undated (b), § C10.16.

for U.S. SSA policy. Future evaluation efforts, however, will require improvements in SSA data if they are to identify more-precise insights into the conditions under which SSA is effective.

CHAPTER THREE

The Debate over the Effectiveness of SSA in Africa

The effects of U.S. SSA have been a perennial subject of debate ever since such programs took their place as an important tool of U.S. foreign policy. This debate is particularly relevant to Africa, and especially now. As shown in Chapter Two, both the amount of SSA that the United States provides to African countries and the number of countries that receive U.S. SSA have increased substantially in the past decade. The United States currently relies predominantly on SSA to achieve its security objectives on the continent, given policymakers' limited appetite for direct military intervention.

This chapter begins by reviewing the debate over how SSA affects conflict dynamics in recipient countries. It then considers the ways in which context might shape the impact of SSA. The chapter explores how the U.S. approach to SSA has changed over time, with significant differences in policy goals and types of SSA apparent between the Cold War and subsequent periods. We then consider the ways in which SSA's effects might depend on partner-nation characteristics, as well as the presence or absence of PKOs. The chapter concludes by developing testable propositions regarding SSA's effects on three types of political violence: civil wars, terrorist attacks, and state repression.

How Might SSA Affect Levels of Violence in Africa?

Proponents of SSA argue that it contributes to partner stability in several positive ways. Most directly, U.S. capacity-building assistance, including equipment and training, strengthens foreign security forces' ability to fight terrorism, deter insurgents, and provide public security. Foreign personnel's exposure to U.S. security institutions via military education, training, and other engagement encourages their adoption of the U.S. ethos of military professionalism, respect for human rights, and civilian supremacy. Furthermore, by building defense institutions, supporting reform efforts, and incentivizing constructive behavior, SSA can improve the conduct of foreign security forces and thus reduce the types of popular grievances that contribute to terrorism or insurgency in the first place. The assumption that these goals are feasible, at least in many circumstances and with the right approaches, underlies most official U.S. SSA planning and guidance.[1]

Critics, however, argue that U.S. SSA can have a range of negative impacts on partner stability. U.S.-provided equipment and combat training might increase recipients' ability and willingness to engage in repression or escalate conflict. Improved training and education might lead security forces to perceive themselves, rightly or wrongly, as more competent than their civilian counterparts and thus best situated to rule the country, even through undemocratic means. The United States could direct SSA to repressive security institutions in the name of strategic interests, sending a signal that U.S. support will continue even in light of future abuses.

All of these arguments about the effects that U.S. SSA can have on political violence in Africa tend to rely on at least one of three main causal pathways: BPC, diffusing behavioral norms, and changing partner incentives. In the rest of this section, we discuss each of these pathways, along with their associated arguments and previous research findings.

Building Partner Capacity

Do partner security institutions use the improved capabilities gained from U.S.-provided equipment and training in ways that contribute to stability and reduce violence?

---

[1] For example, see U.S. Department of State, Bureau of African Affairs, *Security Governance Initiative: 2015 Review*, Washington, D.C., March 2, 2016a; and Waldhauser, 2017b.

SSA's most straightforward effect is to increase the capacity of the partner security forces that receive U.S. equipment, training, and other assistance. Ideally, these forces use this increased capacity to better provide public security and prevent terrorism while adhering to norms of human rights and civilian control of the military. At worst, they enable partner forces to engage in abusive and destabilizing behavior.

Most U.S. SSA is intended to build up security forces' capabilities at the tactical level. There are few systematically collected data that would permit rigorous analysis of whether partners' capabilities do, in fact, improve as a result of U.S.-provided SSA. Nonetheless, there is substantial anecdotal evidence, as well as a limited amount of somewhat more-systematic analysis of selected partners, that suggests that SSA does indeed yield capability gains, at least in the short term.[2] Kenyan forces that received U.S. training and equipment proved capable of conducting a complex amphibious assault against al-Shabaab in Somalia, for example.[3] The United Nations (UN) assessed the Liberian army, which was completely rebuilt with extensive U.S. support, as "well-trained and equipped" despite other shortfalls.[4]

These types of capability improvements might deter would-be terrorists or insurgents from challenging the state, given its growing security capabilities. If more-capable partner security forces are unable to deter challenges from militant groups, improved arms and training could enable security forces to carry out more-effective counterterrorism or counterinsurgency operations, ideally while also reducing unintended killing of civilians, as has been suggested by one quantitative study that examined the record of elite Philippine military forc-

---

2 Christopher Paul, Colin P. Clarke, Beth Grill, Stephanie Young, Jennifer D. P. Moroney, Joe Hogler, and Christine Leah, *What Works Best When Building Partner Capacity and Under What Circumstances?* Santa Monica, Calif.: RAND Corporation, MG-1253/1-OSD, 2013; Seth G. Jones, Andrew Liepman, and Nathan Chandler, *Counterterrorism and Counterinsurgency in Somalia: Assessing the Campaign Against al Shabaab*, Santa Monica, Calif.: RAND Corporation, RR-1539-OSD, 2016.

3 Jones, Liepman, and Chandler, 2016, pp. 47–48.

4 UN Security Council, *Special Report of the Secretary-General on the United Nations Mission in Liberia*, S/2016/968, November 15, 2016, pp. 7–8.

es.[5] In Mali, for example, the military units that received the most-consistent U.S. training and equipment performed well in combat in early 2012, despite the failures of most other Malian units.[6] In Somalia, U.S.-supported African Union (AU) Mission in Somalia forces from Uganda, Kenya, Burundi, and other troop-contributing countries were able to retake most areas that had been controlled by al-Shabaab, although these forces have also come under criticism for misconduct.[7]

There is also the danger, however, that aid increases recipient security forces' ability and willingness to engage in repression, escalatory violence, or other destabilizing behavior. If government forces believe that they can decisively defeat the opposition, the government might have little incentive to rely on peaceful mechanisms of conflict resolution that might entail painful political compromises. For example, U.S. military assistance to Zaire (now the DRC) enabled the Mobuto regime to take a hard line against dissent up until this aid ceased after the Cold War ended.[8] More recently, U.S. military aid to Uganda has allegedly strengthened the regime's ability to suppress political opposition.[9] Even if government forces do not change their behavior, improving their capabilities could inadvertently provoke conflict. If security forces are disproportionately drawn from one ethnic community, increasing their capabilities could shift the interethnic balance of power, causing other ethnic groups to arm themselves in what they believe to be self-defense.[10] In Mali, for instance, many Tuareg per-

---

[5] Joseph H. Felter, *Taking Guns to a Knife Fight: Effective Military Support to COIN*, Carlisle Barracks, Pa.: U.S. Army War College, Senior Service College fellowship project, January 4, 2009, p. 20.

[6] Powelson, 2013, pp. 50–54.

[7] Jones, Liepman, and Chandler, 2016; Paul D. Williams with Abdirashid Hashi, *Exit Strategy Challenges for the AU Mission in Somalia*, Mogadishu, Somalia: Heritage Institute for Policy Studies, February 2016.

[8] Steven Metz, *Reform, Conflict, and Security in Zaire*, Carlisle Barracks, Pa.: U.S. Army War College, Strategic Studies Institute, June 5, 1996, pp. 8–13.

[9] Ty McCormick, "Is the U.S. Military Propping Up Uganda's 'Elected' Autocrat?" *Foreign Policy*, February 18, 2016.

[10] Barry R. Posen, "The Security Dilemma and Ethnic Conflict," *Survival*, Vol. 35, No. 1, Spring 1993, pp. 27–47.

ceived U.S. SSA as favoring southern ethnic groups, a potential factor in the Tuareg uprising in 2012.[11]

SSA can also be diverted to insurgent, criminal, or terrorist groups, through theft, through capture, on the black market, or in the form of defections. In Mali, elite units trained and equipped by the United States defected to antigovernment Tuareg rebels in 2012, "taking troops, guns, trucks, and their newfound skills" along with them.[12] In Somalia, al-Shabaab has obtained equipment provided to U.S.-supported peacekeeping troops both through capture and on the black market.[13] In 2014, Libyan militias seized U.S.-provided weapons and vehicles from a base outside Tripoli.[14] This is a particular concern for many African countries, which often suffer from corruption and mismanagement in their security institutions.[15] In other cases, SSA recipients might deliberately divert aid to progovernment militias responsible for extrajudicial killings and other abuses.[16] In Burundi, for instance, there have been concerns that recipients of U.S. SSA were involved in arming the progovernment Imbonerakure militia, which has been implicated in serious human-rights abuses.[17]

---

[11] David Gutelius, "Islam in Northern Mali and the War on Terror," *Journal of Contemporary African Studies*, Vol. 25, No. 1, 2007, p. 66.

[12] Adam Nossiter, Eric Schmitt, and Mark Mazzetti, "French Strikes in Mali Supplant Caution of U.S.," *New York Times*, January 13, 2013.

[13] Caleb Weiss, "Shabaab Releases Photos from Captured African Union Base," *Threat Matrix*, January 21, 2016; Nicolas Florquin and Jonah Leff, "Across Conflict Zones: Ammunition Profiling," in *Small Arms Survey 2014: Women and Guns*, Geneva: Small Arms Survey, 2014, pp. 200–201.

[14] Eric Schmitt, "U.S. Training Elite Antiterror Troops in Four African Nations," *New York Times*, May 26, 2014.

[15] Aryn Baker, "Corruption in Military Defense Spending Could Be Behind Rise in Africa Terror Attacks," *Time*, January 19, 2016.

[16] Oeindrila Dube and Suresh Naidu, "Bases, Bullets, and Ballots: The Effect of US Military Aid on Political Conflict in Colombia," *Journal of Politics*, Vol. 77, No. 1, January 2015, pp. 249–267; Neil J. Mitchell, Sabine C. Carey, and Christopher K. Butler, "The Impact of Pro-Government Militias on Human Rights Violations," *International Interactions*, Vol. 40, No. 5, 2014, pp. 812–836.

[17] Alexis Arieff, *Burundi's Electoral Crisis: In Brief*, Washington, D.C.: Congressional Research Service, R44018, May 14, 2015, p. 10.

The United States also provides PME, as well as training, to build partner capacity in logistics, intelligence, operational planning, and other higher-level security functions, as discussed in Chapter Two. This type of capacity building, although less directly applicable to tactical combat, can affect operational effectiveness, deterrence, and interethnic power relations in the same way as military equipment can. Unlike tactical assistance in the form of equipment, however, this type of SSA increases exclusively what Jesse Dillon Savage and Jonathan Caverley call security forces' "human capital," meaning both their social status and their professional knowledge and technical skills.[18] Increasing the capacity of partner military personnel relative to their civilian counterparts can make it harder for the latter to be held accountable for destabilizing actions because the country's civilian leadership (as well as the United States) might be reluctant to punish military actors on whose competence they rely. It could also lead military officers to see themselves as more competent and therefore deserving of political power than civilian officials, increasing the risk of a coup.[19]

DIB is specifically intended to build partner security institutions' ability to serve as a stabilizing force by "improving civilian control of the military, building respect for the rule of law, and improving military professionalism."[20] Unlike other forms of SSA, it does not focus on building partner forces' "operational readiness or tactical capabilities."[21] This type of SSA is more likely to improve the personnel management, strategic planning, and accountability mechanisms that underlie security force performance. Because it seeks to build the capacity of both military and civilian security actors, this form of aid is less likely than others to shift power toward the former in any destabilizing way. Some analysts argue that supporting this type of SSA is the most appropriate

---

18 Savage and Caverley, 2017, p. 545.

19 Savage and Caverley, 2017, pp. 545–546.

20 Thomas W. Ross, "Defining the Discipline in Theory and Practice," in Alexandra Kerr and Michael Miklaucic, eds., *Effective, Legitimate, Secure: Insights for Defense Institution Building*, Washington, D.C.: Center for Complex Operations, Institute for National Strategic Studies, National Defense University, 2017, p. 24.

21 McNerney, Johnson, et al., 2016, p. x.

response to concerns raised about the dangers of providing equipment or combat-focused training to dysfunctional partner security institutions.[22] Nevertheless, U.S. efforts to support DIB are still relatively new and thus difficult to evaluate. Other donors' similar efforts have, at times, been criticized as having unrealistic goals given the significant barriers to institutional change in poorly governed states.[23]

Another limitation on the effectiveness of SSA is the timescale required for implementation. On the U.S. side, there are "long lead times for ordering, producing, and delivering" equipment following SSA allocation decisions.[24] In addition, it often takes years for partner forces to fully train up and field U.S.-provided equipment after it is delivered, and delays are common because recipients underestimate the complexity of new equipment and the scale and duration of technical training requirements.[25] PME is similarly expected to have an effect on partner capacity only after foreign officers return home and have the opportunity to put their training to use as they move up through the ranks. The experience of U.S. and others' efforts to support SSR and DIB suggest that these forms of SSA also take years to bear fruit.[26]

Importantly, one major critique of U.S. SSA holds that it is not effective at BPC in the first place. There are some indications that this is particularly true in countries that suffer from poor governance and low levels of economic development, as is common in Africa.[27] There are numerous anecdotes of the United States providing equipment and training that partner forces have been unable to effectively use. For

---

[22] Rachel Kleinfeld, "Fragility and Security Sector Reform," Washington, D.C.: U.S. Institute of Peace, September 27, 2016.

[23] Albrecht Schnabel, "Ideal Requirements Versus Real Environments in Security Sector Reform," in Hans Born and Albrecht Schnabel, eds., *Security Sector Reform in Challenging Environments*, Geneva: Geneva Centre for the Democratic Control of Armed Forces, 2009, pp. 3–38.

[24] Bruce E. Arlinghaus, *Military Development in Africa: The Political and Economic Risks of Arms Transfers*, Boulder, Colo.: Westview Press, 1984, p. 74.

[25] Arlinghaus, 1984, pp. 74–75.

[26] McNerney, Johnson, et al., 2016, p. 20.

[27] McNerney, O'Mahony, et al., 2014, pp. xiv–xv.

example, during the Cold War, the United States transferred some battle tanks to Sudan; only upon delivery was it discovered that they were too heavy for the Sudanese to move using their existing transportation infrastructure.[28] More recently, Nigeria has struggled to maintain U.S. transport planes, and Liberia has failed to keep most of its U.S.-provided military vehicles operational.[29] Yet even in these and other cases in which SSA is ineffective in BPC, SSA might still have positive or negative effects by either influencing partners' norms or changing their incentives, as discussed next.

Transmission of Norms

Does attendance at U.S. military schools and training alongside U.S. forces lead partner security personnel to adopt an ethos that prioritizes military professionalism, adherence to human-rights norms, and respect for civilian control of the military?

In 2013, following a military coup and insurgent gains in Mali, the lead U.S. military commander in Africa declared that, in hindsight, U.S. training for Malian troops should have focused more on "values, ethics, and a military ethos," rather than "almost exclusively on tactical or technical matters."[30] The commander's regret accords strongly with the view that SSA can reduce political violence in partner states via the transmission of U.S. norms to foreign security forces.

Those who argue the importance of transmission of norms often place particular emphasis on foreign attendance at U.S. PME institutions through the IMET program.[31] Similar arguments have also been made about the importance of norm transmission via education for

---

[28] Arlinghaus, 1984, p. 68.

[29] Douglas Farah, "U.S. to Help Nigeria Revamp Its Armed Forces," *Washington Post*, April 29, 2000; Alec Lloyd, "U.S. Air Forces Africa Help Nigerian C-130 Fly Again," U.S. Africa Command, September 1, 2009; McNerney, Johnson, et al., 2016, p. 67.

[30] "Mali Crisis: US Admits Mistakes in Training Local Troops," *BBC*, January 25, 2013.

[31] Although the primary model used in this report does not include measures of foreign students' course attendance, in the aggregate measures of SSA funding in the model, we do include the extent of U.S. assistance in the form of professional military education for foreign students. An alternative model discussed in Appendix C does, however, include measures of foreign students' course attendance.

world leaders more broadly. One recent study found that leaders who attended Western universities "significantly and substantively improve a country's democratization prospects," with the transmission of social preferences for democracy as a posited primary cause.[32]

Transmission of U.S. norms is argued to depend on the "depth and breadth of social interactions [and] the sharing of a sense of community" between foreign participants and their American hosts. The impact of transmission of norms then depends on the extent to which foreign graduates ascend to influential positions back home following program completion.[33] One academic highlighted the case of the U.S.-trained Nigerian General Abdulsalami Abubakar, who ended military rule and quickly ushered in democratic elections after he came to power in 1998, as an example of how diffusion of American norms via military training can lead to positive civil–military outcomes abroad.[34]

In some cases, the transfer of U.S. norms to foreign security forces is meant to be direct. U.S. education programs include courses on human rights, adherence to the laws of war, and military leadership that are intended to actively impart a specific ethos of military professionalism. More broadly, some argue that living and studying alongside U.S. military forces and being surrounded by American culture, particularly for prolonged periods of time, encourage democratic values through a more diffuse and immersive transmission process.[35]

Others have argued that transmission of norms is likely to be weak because foreign officers are already steeped in their own countries' norms concerning military conduct. Furthermore, U.S. military norms might be incompatible or even destabilizing in some contexts. Foreign

---

32 Thomas Gift and Daniel Krcmaric, "Who Democratizes? Western-Educated Leaders and Regime Transitions," *Journal of Conflict Resolution*, Vol. 61, No. 3, 2017, pp. 671–701.

33 Carol Atkinson, "Does Soft Power Matter? A Comparative Analysis of Student Exchange Programs 1980–2006," *Foreign Policy Analysis*, Vol. 6, No. 1, January 2010, pp. 1–22.

34 Jean Herskovits, professor of history, State University of New York, *The Nigerian Transition and the Future of U.S. Policy*, testimony before the U.S. Senate Committee on Foreign Relations, 106th Congress, 1st session, November 4, 1999.

35 Tomislav Z. Ruby and Douglas Gibler, "US Professional Military Education and Democratization Abroad," *European Journal of International Relations*, Vol. 16, No. 3, 2010, pp. 339–364; Atkinson, 2010.

officers from autocratic states might find it impossible to adhere to norms concerning protection of the rule of law and human rights while maintaining military deference to civilian leadership, at least in cases in which the country's civilian leaders themselves act against democratic or human rights. Such dilemmas might render U.S. norms irrelevant or might contribute to the likelihood of military coups against oppressive leaders. The American military ethos of professionalism and strong corporate identity might similarly be destabilizing if the military comes to see itself as more competent or virtuous than civilian leaders.[36]

Like with BPC, it would take time for transmission of norms to affect partner security forces' overall behavior because security officials who absorb U.S. norms gain the clout needed to influence their comrades and institute changes back home.

Changing Partner Incentives

Do U.S. policy decisions on who does and does not receive SSA, and under what conditions, create incentives for partner nations to behave well or poorly?

The final mechanism by which SSA might affect political violence is by changing the incentives faced by security forces, political leaders, and other actors in recipient states. The degree to which U.S. SSA might change foreign states' behavior is largely driven by U.S. policies on which states receive it, the amount and type of SSA that different states receive, and the conditions under which they can expect continued assistance. The United States can attempt to influence partner-nation behavior by allocating SSA to those partner nations that are most committed to taking constructive and cooperative action to reduce political violence and institute needed security reforms. Alternatively, the United States can cut off SSA to partners, whether entire states or specific security actors, that take destabilizing actions.

Besides executive-branch efforts to influence partner behavior through selective incentives, Congress has passed some laws designed to incentivize constructive partner behavior via the allocation of SSA.

---

[36] Savage and Caverley, 2017, pp. 544–545.

In 1974, Congress passed a blanket restriction, known as Section 502B, on U.S. assistance to any country that has engaged in a "consistent pattern of gross violations of internationally recognized human rights."[37] Twelve years later, Congress passed legislation, known as the "coup provision," to bar the State Department from providing SSA to any country whose elected government is deposed by a military coup, at least until democracy is restored.[38] The Leahy laws, passed in the late 1990s, prohibit the United States from providing training and certain other types of SSA to foreign security forces "where there is credible evidence that a unit had committed gross violations of human rights."[39] Recent legislation has expanded this restriction to cover all types of U.S. SSA. It also created a path for an offending unit to become eligible again for aid if offending personnel are brought to justice.[40]

The executive-branch record in implementing these legislative requirements is mixed, although it has generally followed statutory SSA restrictions, at least those that are more narrowly targeted and do not conflict with other overriding interests. Section 502B remains law, but it has rarely, if ever, been invoked in its more than four decades of existence.[41] In contrast, the Leahy restrictions have been institutionalized, with the State Department establishing a multistage process and centralized database that it uses to vet all foreign security forces subject to the Leahy laws.[42] Since the coup provision was established in 1986,

---

[37] John W. Dietrich, "U.S. Human Rights Policy in the Post–Cold War Era," *Political Science Quarterly*, Vol. 121, No. 2, Summer 2006, p. 277. Public Law 93-559, Foreign Assistance Act of 1974, December 30, 1974, added Section 502B to Public Law 87-195, Foreign Assistance Act of 1961, September 4, 1961.

[38] Larry Hanauer and Stephanie Pezard, *Security Cooperation Amidst Political Uncertainty: An Agenda for Future Research*, Santa Monica, Calif.: RAND Corporation, WR-1052, 2014, p. 18.

[39] Nina M. Serafino, June S. Beittel, Lauren Ploch Blanchard, and Liana Rosen, "Leahy Law," *Human Rights Provisions and Security Assistance: Issue Overview*, Washington, D.C.: Congressional Research Service, R43361, January 29, 2014, p. 3.

[40] Serafino et al., 2014.

[41] Serafino et al., 2014, p. 3.

[42] Michael J. McNerney, Jonah Blank, Becca Wasser, Jeremy Boback, and Alexander Stephenson, *Improving Implementation of the Department of Defense Leahy Law*, Santa

successive presidential administrations have adhered to it in nearly all cases in which it applied, with a few exceptions discussed in the next section.

Executive-branch officials have also, at times, suspended security aid or threatened to do so in attempts to deter state repression or defuse political crises in partner nations before they escalate to civil war. During Burkina Faso's 2014–2015 coup attempts and political crises, for example, the Obama administration repeatedly voiced its support for a peaceful democratic transition and called on the security forces to refrain from violence, making it clear that either an armed escalation or establishment of military rule would result in a cutoff of SSA.[43] The United States canceled the delivery of military helicopters to Nigeria in 2014, following reports that the Nigerian army had engaged in mass killings of civilians during the campaign against Boko Haram.[44] In 2015, the United States similarly suspended SSA to Burundi because of security forces' involvement in human-rights abuses.[45]

Of course, strengthening a partner state's internal stability might not be the highest-priority consideration for the United States when it makes SSA allocation decisions. Numerous other U.S. interests, such as containing the spread of communism, defeating transnational terrorist groups, securing access to basing rights, and preventing interstate conflict, have, at times, driven SSA decisions. In "Changes in U.S. Security Sector Assistance Policy over Time," in the next section, we

---

Monica, Calif.: RAND Corporation, RR-1737-OSD, 2017. The application of the Leahy restrictions has, at times, led to protests by recipient states, such as Nigeria (Ashish Kumar Sen, "Nigerian President Slams US Law," Atlantic Council, July 22, 2015).

[43] J. C. Finley, "White House Weighs In on Situation in Burkina Faso," UPI, October 30, 2014; "Burkina Faso's Lt Col Isaac Zida Named Prime Minister," *BBC*, November 19, 2014; "Burkina Faso Military Installs General as New Head of State After Coup," Associated Press, September 17, 2015; Craig Whitlock, "Coup Leader in Burkina Faso Received U.S. Military Training," *Washington Post*, November 3, 2014.

[44] Helene Cooper, "Rifts Between U.S. and Nigeria Impeding Fight Against Boko Haram," *New York Times*, January 24, 2015.

[45] U.S. Department of State, Bureau of Counterterrorism and Countering Violent Extremism, "Country Reports: Africa Overview," in *Country Reports on Terrorism 2015*, Washington, D.C., June 2, 2016b.

discuss the evolution of U.S. strategic interests and their role in overriding concerns about SSA's effects on internal political violence.

Under certain circumstances, U.S. SSA decisions might, in fact, create incentives for partner nations to behave in counterproductive ways. This is particularly the case when a specific U.S. strategic interest, such as counterterrorism, is seen to be driving U.S. decisions on SSA. If a partner nation commits human-rights abuses in the name of this interest and continues to receive U.S. SSA, the partner nation could interpret this as a signal that the United States tolerates or supports such actions, lowering the bar for engaging in repression in the future.[46] Every year, the State Department releases reports on human-rights abuses committed by partner governments that nevertheless continue to receive aid. This disconnect is readily apparent to recipients. One former Nigerian diplomat, for instance, protested a U.S. decision to suspend delivery of military equipment by referring to the continued provision of SSA to other abusive regimes.[47] Some analysts have argued that SSA can create problems of moral hazard for recipients. Partner nations that depend on U.S. SSA and know that this aid is primarily motivated by continued instability within their borders might have little incentive to definitively address the sources of that instability, preferring to keep it at a manageable level to ensure that aid continues to flow.[48] Some observers have charged that Kenya, for instance, has engaged in precisely such practices.[49]

---

[46] Cédric Jourde, "The International Relations of Small Neoauthoritarian States: Islamism, Warlordism, and the Framing of Stability," *International Studies Quarterly*, Vol. 51, No. 2, June 2007, pp. 481–503; Patricia L. Sullivan, Brock F. Tessman, and Xiaojun Li, "US Military Aid and Recipient State Cooperation," *Foreign Policy Analysis*, Vol. 7, No. 3, July 2011, pp. 275–294.

[47] Joe Keshi, "America–Nigeria Troubled Relations," *Vanguard*, October 24, 2014. Also see Dietrich, 2006, p. 292.

[48] Navin A. Bapat, "Transnational Terrorism, US Military Aid, and the Incentive to Misrepresent," *Journal of Peace Research*, Vol. 48, No. 3, 2011, pp. 308–318; Andrew Boutton, "Of Terrorism and Revenue: Why Foreign Aid Exacerbates Terrorism in Personalist Regimes," *Conflict Management and Peace Science*, December 21, 2016.

[49] Clint Watts, Jacob Shapiro, and Vahid Brown, *Al-Qa'ida's (Mis)Adventures in the Horn of Africa*, West Point, N.Y.: Combating Terrorism Center at West Point, July 2, 2007, pp. 61–62, 65.

Some have contended that efforts to incentivize better partner behavior can also, at times, conflict with efforts to spread U.S. norms. The former head of U.S. Special Operations Command expressed this view when he testified to Congress that the Leahy restrictions might actually have counterproductive results. These restrictions, he argued, prevent the United States from conducting training on human-rights issues and encouraging the adoption of professional norms by the types of abusive foreign security forces that probably need such engagement the most.[50] Conversely, others who seek the strengthening of Leahy restrictions contend that such arguments are disingenuous.[51] Although this argument has not convinced Congress to relax the Leahy laws, a similar logic underpins congressional decisions to allow certain problematic countries to continue to receive training under the Expanded IMET (E-IMET) program, which avoids tactical subjects and includes a greater focus than IMET does on human rights.[52]

U.S. policies that restrict the provision of SSA to abusive security forces or military-led regimes are most directly focused on reducing two types of political violence: state repression and coup attempts. Other SSA allocation decisions, such as encouraging partner states to undertake reforms as part of a broader SSA package (as in postconflict Liberia or in the ongoing Security Governance Initiative [SGI]), might incentivize partners to improve their security institutions in ways that reduce political violence more generally. The strength of all these incentives, however, depends significantly on whether the United States can

---

[50] Phil Stewart, "U.S. Commander Seeks to Ease Human-Rights Rules That Limit Training," Reuters, March 6, 2013. For similar arguments, also see Mark Moyar, *Aid for Elites: Building Partner Nations and Ending Poverty Through Human Capital*, New York: Cambridge University Press, 2016, and David Passage, *The United States and Colombia: Untying the Gordian Knot*, Carlisle, Pa.: Strategic Studies Institute, U.S. Army War College, March 2000, p. 26.

[51] See, for example, Edward McKinney, "Don't Bend the Law to Fight Terror in Nigeria," *National Interest*, June 2, 2016.

[52] In 2012, the list of African countries allowed PKOs and E-IMET but barred from regular IMET consisted of Angola, Cameroon, the Central African Republic, Chad, Cote d'Ivoire, Guinea, and Zimbabwe (Pub. L. 112-74, Consolidated Appropriations Act, 2012, Section 7043[d], Expanded International Military Education and Training, December 23, 2011).

credibly threaten to cut aid. This depends, in turn, on whether U.S. SSA is motivated primarily by humanitarian and stabilization concerns or, conversely, by the need to secure recipient-state cooperation in service of some other overriding U.S. national interest. In the next section, we discuss the motivations for U.S. SSA and the ways in which they changed during and after the Cold War.

How Might Context Affect the Impact of SSA?

It is, of course, highly unlikely that SSA has had uniform effects throughout Africa over a span of several decades. It might be more or less effective depending on the context—and, indeed, it might have a favorable impact in some cases and counterproductive effects in others. Understanding these contextual influences through statistical models requires more than simply "controlling" for the independent effects of context. We must look at the interaction of SSA and numerous contextual variables. According to prior analyses of SSA, three types of factors are likely to be particularly influential in shaping SSA's mode of delivery and ultimate impact: the superpower competition of the Cold War, the presence of PKOs at the time SSA is implemented, and the governance structures of the partner nations.

Changes in U.S. SSA Policy over Time

American policies governing the allocation and implementation of SSA do not remain static. At various times, strategic factors could lead the United States to emphasize some goals over others. Consequently, there is no reason to believe that the effects of SSA will be consistent over time. No other single factor has shaped U.S. SSA policy more than the Cold War and its abrupt end in 1991.[53]

---

[53] This is also true of U.S. policy on foreign aid more generally. Several studies have documented the ways in which U.S. foreign aid policy changed dramatically in the post–Cold War era. These have generally concluded that U.S. aid became more effective in supporting economic growth, promoting democracy, and deterring coups after the Cold War ended (David H. Bearce and Daniel C. Tirone, "Foreign Aid Effectiveness and the Strategic Goals of Donor Governments," *Journal of Politics*, Vol. 72, No. 3, July 2010, pp. 837–851; Takaaki

Containing the spread of Soviet influence and communism was the overriding U.S. concern behind U.S. SSA allocation decisions during much of the Cold War.[54] The U.S. view toward SSA recipients during this period was that "government repression was unfortunate but sometimes inevitable in countries dealing with subversive elements."[55] Early congressional restrictions on SSA use focused on terminating military aid to any countries that provide strategically important items, especially armaments, to members of the Soviet bloc.[56] Accordingly, the primary norms and attitudes that U.S. training was intended to impart to foreign military officers from developing countries during this period were an overall pro-American orientation and antipathy toward communism.[57] Not until 1978 did Congress add encouraging respect for human rights to the list of objectives for the IMET program. Even then, DoD did little to incorporate human rights into course content, choosing only to include it as one of 11 topics covered in an elective course for IMET trainees.[58]

Congressional concerns about abuses committed by U.S.-supported security forces, especially in Latin America, led to the passage of restrictions on U.S. SSA to foreign police forces in 1974 and the

---

Masaki, "*Coups d'État* and Foreign Aid," *World Development*, Vol. 79, March 2016, p. 60; Nikolay Marinov and Hein Goemans, "Coups and Democracy," *British Journal of Political Science*, Vol. 44, No. 4, October 2014, pp. 799–825).

[54] Donald Stoker, "The Evolution of Foreign Military Advising and Assistance, 1815–2005," in Kendall D. Gott and Michael G. Brooks, eds., *Security Assistance: U.S. and International Historical Perspectives—The Proceedings of the Combat Studies Institute 2006 Military History Symposium*, Fort Leavenworth, Kan.: Combat Studies Institute Press, 2006, pp. 36–37.

[55] Seth G. Jones, Olga Oliker, Peter Chalk, C. Christine Fair, Rollie Lal, and James Dobbins, *Securing Tyrants or Fostering Reform? U.S. Internal Security Assistance to Repressive and Transitioning Regimes*, Santa Monica, Calif.: RAND Corporation, MG-550-OSI, 2006, p. 15.

[56] Mutual Security Agency, *Mutual Defense Assistance Control Act of 1951: Public Law 213—82d Congress: First Report to Congress*, Vols. 1–8, Washington, D.C., October 15, 1952.

[57] John Samuel Fitch, "The Political Impact of U.S. Military Aid to Latin America," *Armed Forces and Society*, Vol. 5, No. 3, 1979, pp. 360–386.

[58] John Samuel Fitch, "Human Rights and the U.S. Military Training Program: Alternatives for Latin America," *Human Rights Quarterly*, Vol. 3, No. 4, November 1981, pp. 65–66, 68.

eventual passage of the coup provision in the subsequent decade.[59] Yet even during the Carter administration, which elevated the importance of human rights in U.S. policy, the White House "elected to use arms sales as a major weapon to challenge Soviet intrusion and influence into Africa," despite the problematic records of many recipient states.[60] This pattern continued during the Reagan administration as well.[61]

The end of the Cold War marked an opening for other U.S. interests to shape policy on SSA in Africa. In 1990, the U.S. Assistant Secretary of State for African Affairs "announced that democratization would join economic reform and human rights as a condition for future US assistance," guidance that was followed in aid allocation decisions in the subsequent two years.[62] The E-IMET program was established in 1991 to increase the proportion of SSA training that focused on human rights, rule of law, and civilian control of the military.[63] The number of multilateral peacekeeping missions in Africa rose substantially as the former Cold War rivals took a more cooperative approach to conflict management in the continent under the auspices of the UN.[64] This was a dramatic change from the previous pattern in which the United States and its Cold War rivals often provided assistance to warring parties on opposite sides of a conflict in such countries as Angola and the DRC.[65]

Despite policy changes in favor of direct humanitarian intervention in Africa after the end of the Cold War, the United States soon

---

[59] Jones, Oliker, et al., 2006, pp. 11–13.

[60] Arlinghaus, 1984, p. 39.

[61] Arlinghaus, 1984, p. 39.

[62] Letitia Lawson, "External Democracy Promotion in Africa: Another False Start?" *Commonwealth and Comparative Politics*, Vol. 37, No. 1, 1999, p. 5.

[63] Richard F. Grimmett, *International Military Education and Training Program*, Washington, D.C.: Congressional Research Service, RS20506, October 28, 2004.

[64] Letitia Lawson, "U.S. Africa Policy Since the Cold War," *Strategic Insights*, Vol. 6, No. 1, January 2007.

[65] See, for example, U.S. Department of State, Office of the Historian, "The Congo, Decolonization, and the Cold War: 1960–1965," undated (c); and U.S. Department of State, Office of the Historian, "The Angola Crisis: 1974–75," undated (b).

cooled to this prospect, particularly following its failed 1993–1994 mission in Somalia.[66] The continued outbreak of civil war on the continent, including genocide in Rwanda in 1994, prompted the Clinton administration to call instead for an increase in African-led, U.S.-supported regional peacekeeping efforts.[67] This pattern of support for African peacekeepers, as well as host-nation security forces, while minimizing U.S. troop involvement has continued through the present.

The September 11, 2001, attacks immediately elevated counterterrorism and the defeat of al Qaeda to the top of U.S. policy goals, including for SSA. The United States greatly expanded its SSA allocation to Africa and reoriented much of its stabilization and peacekeeping-focused SSA toward counterterrorism concerns. The George W. Bush administration quickly resumed SSA to Algeria, which had previously been barred under the coup provision.[68] The amount of SSA provided to African countries increased significantly beginning around 2005, the same year in which the United States established the Trans-Sahara Counterterrorism Partnership (TSCTP) to address the threat of al Qaeda in northwest Africa. This was followed by the similar deepening of SSA relationships to counter al-Shabaab in east Africa and later Boko Haram in west Africa.

The type of SSA provided has also changed over time. During the Cold War, the great majority of U.S. SSA to Africa took the form of military equipment and equipment-related training. This fell significantly after the end of the Cold War as FMF was eventually replaced by the PKO account as the largest source of SSA in the continent.[69]

---

[66] Emmanuel K. Aning, "African Crisis Response Initiative and the New African Security (Dis)order," *African Journal of Political Science*, Vol. 6, No. 1, 2001, pp. 47–48.

[67] Aning, 2001, p. 48.

[68] This and SSA provision to military-led governments in Pakistan and, later, in Egypt have been the only exceptions made to the coup provision following the end of the Cold War. In contrast, the United States has suspended SSA because of military coups in the following countries in Africa: Algeria (1991), Nigeria (1993 and 1999), Mauritania (2008), Madagascar (2009), and Mali (2012) ("Congressional Control of Foreign Assistance to Post-Coup States: Assessing Executive Compliance from Honduras to Egypt," *Harvard Law Review*, Vol. 127, No. 8, June 20, 2014, pp. 2499–2520).

[69] USAID, 2016.

IMET continued, with an additional focus on nontechnical instruction on human rights and other subjects, and was joined by smaller SSA programs focused on BPC at both the tactical and the institutional levels. Although it is still small, a growing amount of SSA has focused on DIB and improving security sector oversight and accountability, with the creation of the SGI in 2014 being the latest manifestation of this trend.

Peacekeeping Environments

One of the most-important factors affecting the impact of U.S. SSA in Africa is whether assistance is provided in the context of a UN PKO. This is particularly true in the period since the end of the Cold War, when most PKOs have occurred. There have been 29 UN peacekeeping missions in Africa, more than in any other region. Although a small minority of these were focused solely on maintaining a physical buffer between warring parties, most peacekeeping missions were charged with improving internal security conditions within a country and included technical assistance to the host government. Table 3.1 lists the 25 UN peacekeeping missions that fall into this second category. Six of these are still ongoing.[70]

The SSR paradigm emerged in the 1990s in response to the need for overhaul of security institutions in the wake of democratic transitions and in the context of large-scale, complex PKOs.[71] The SSR and related literatures suggest several potential reasons U.S. SSA might have different effects in peacekeeping contexts. The presence of peacekeeping troops, often in combination with foreign police and military advisers, entails increased external oversight of host-nation secu-

---

[70] This analysis focused exclusively on UN PKOs, excluding those led by the AU or other entities. UN PKOs are conducted in accordance with UN mandates and are supervised by the UN Security Council and other UN entities. The same dynamics that appear in UN operations might or might not be replicated in operations undertaken by other actors, some of which resemble traditional counterinsurgency more than they resemble UN-led PKOs.

[71] The canonical work on SSR remains Organisation for Economic Co-operation and Development (OECD), *The OECD DAC Handbook on Security System Reform: Supporting Security and Justice*, Paris: Organisation for Economic Co-operation and Development, Development Assistance Committee, February 25, 2008.

Table 3.1
United Nations Peacekeeping Operations in Africa

Nation	Period	Mission
Republic of the Congo	1960–1964	UN Operation in the Congo (originally Organisation des Nations Unies au Congo, or ONUC)
Namibia	1989–1990	UN Transition Assistance Group (UNTAG)
Angola	1989–1991	UN Angola Verification Mission (UNAVEM) I
Angola	1991–1994	UNAVEM II
Somalia	1992–1993	UN Operation in Somalia (UNOSOM) I & II
Mozambique	1992–1994	UN Operation in Mozambique (UNOMOZ)
Somalia	1993–1995	UNOSOM II
Liberia	1993–1997	UN Observer Mission in Liberia (UNOMIL)
Rwanda	1993–1996	UN Assistance Mission for Rwanda (UNAMIR)
Angola	1995–1997	UNAVEM III
Angola	1997–1999	UN Observer Mission in Angola (Mission d'Observation des Nations Unies à l'Angola, or MONUA)
CAR	1998–2000	UN Mission in CAR (Mission des Nations Unies en République Centrafricaine, or MINURCA)
Sierra Leone	1998–1999	UN Observer Mission in Sierra Leone (UNOMSIL)
Sierra Leone	1999–2006	UN Mission in Sierra Leone (UNAMSIL)
DRC	1999–2010	UN Organization Mission in the DRC (Mission de l'Organisation des Nations unies pour la stabilisation en République démocratique du Congo, or MONUSCO)
Liberia	2003–present	UN Mission in Liberia (UNMIL)
Burundi	2004–2006	UN Operation in Burundi (ONUB)
Cote d'Ivoire	2004–2017	UN Operation in Côte d'Ivoire (Opération des Nations Unies en Côte d'Ivoire, or ONUCI)
Sudan	2005–2011	UN Mission in Sudan (UNMIS)
CAR and Chad	2007–2010	UN Mission in CAR and Chad (MINURCAT)
Sudan	2007–present	AU–UN Mission in Darfur (UNAMID)

Table 3.1—Continued

Nation	Period	Mission
DRC	2010–present	UN Organization Stabilization Mission in the DRC (Mission de l'Organisation des Nations unies pour la stabilisation en République démocratique du Congo, or MONUSCO)
South Sudan	2011–present	UN Mission in South Sudan (UNMISS)
Mali	2013–present	UN Multidimensional Integrated Stabilization Mission in Mali (Mission multidimensionnelle intégrée des Nations unies pour la stabilization au Mali, or MINUSMA)
CAR	2014–present	UN Multidimensional Integrated Stabilization Mission in CAR (MINUSCA)

NOTE: CAR = Central African Republic.

rity forces and increased external involvement in how recipients utilize SSA. This has been particularly the case since 2000, after an internal UN review of PKOs recommended that future UN missions involve greater focus on the restructuring and reform of host-nation security institutions.[72]

At times, U.S. SSA provided in peacekeeping contexts (including SSA that is counted in the USAID Greenbook as allocated to the host country) actually goes to security forces from contributing countries, which are often more capable and less predatory than the host-nation security forces, whose failures led to the establishment of a peacekeeping mission in the first place. Peacekeeping environments also generally feature more-regular and more-intense contact between host-nation forces and external security providers, such as troop contributors, contractors, and U.S. personnel implementing SSA, allowing for greater development of skills and diffusion of norms.

---

[72] UN General Assembly Security Council, *Report of the Panel on United Nations Peace Operations* (commonly known as the Brahimi Report), A/55/305–S/2000/809, August 1, 2000, pp. 3, 5, 7, 20. For a broader discussion of SSA's role in PKOs, see Monica Duffy Toft, *Securing the Peace: The Durable Settlement of Civil Wars*, Princeton, N.J.: Princeton University Press, 2010, pp. 22–24.

The U.S. policy goals that drive the provision of SSA in peacekeeping environments are often different from the policy goals that determine SSA decisions elsewhere. U.S. SSA in these contexts generally supports the peacekeeping mandate of reducing internal political violence and is less likely to be driven by other U.S. strategic interests. Similarly, U.S. SSA provided in peacekeeping environments tends less toward combat-oriented military equipment and more toward training and DIB.

The U.S. support of UN peacekeeping efforts in Liberia following the end of that country's civil war is a prominent example of this type of SSA. U.S. foreign policy at the time was increasingly focused on fighting transnational terrorism, although Liberia was of little or no importance in this effort.[73] Nevertheless, from 2003 to 2010, the United States undertook the task of completely rebuilding the Liberian armed forces and defense ministry in conjunction with the UN peacekeeping mission. U.S. decisions surrounding the size and organization of the new army, as well as the vetting and training of recruits, were driven by conflict-prevention concerns and deliberately avoided creating the types of elite, counterterrorism-focused units that the United States was supporting elsewhere.[74] Recent research suggests that SSA was successful in Liberia precisely because it was conducted in conjunction with a PKO.[75]

The Effects of Local Governance

Research on foreign aid suggests that assistance to particular types of recipient governments, such as personalist dictatorships or military

---

[73] George W. Bush, *The National Security Strategy of the United States of America*, Washington, D.C.: Executive Office of the President, September 2002; U.S. Department of State, Office of the Coordinator for Counterterrorism, *Country Reports on Terrorism 2007*, April 2008, pp. 19–20.

[74] McFate, 2013, pp. 49–52.

[75] Sabrina M. Karim and William A. Wagstaff, "Keeping the Peace After Peacekeeping: How Peacekeepers Resolve the Security Dilemma in Post-Conflict States," unpublished paper.

regimes, is more likely to be misused than aid to democracies.[76] States with higher bureaucratic capacity and quality of governance, such as Botswana, conversely, might be more likely to use aid in constructive ways.[77] In states with lower capacity for governance, aid might instead weaken institutions by encouraging passivity and increasing opportunities for corruption.[78] One recent RAND study found that SSA effectiveness depends in part on the quality of partner-nation governance and infrastructure development.[79] Another found that, although U.S. SSA generally contributed to a reduction in recipient-state fragility, this did not hold for the types of poorly governed and highly fragile states that were more common in Africa.[80]

Arguments to Be Tested

This review of extant theoretical and empirical (almost entirely qualitative) analyses of SSA reveals little consensus about the likely net impact of SSA in Africa. There are sound deductive reasons for anticipating both positive and negative outcomes. There are also innumerable individual cases that lend some credence to the arguments of both SSA optimists and pessimists. Clearly, the field would benefit from an overall accounting of U.S.-provided SSA's net impact on the continent.

Chapters Four and Five describe our analyses of the impact that U.S. SSA has on three measurable types of political violence in Africa:

---

[76] Boutton, 2016; Brian Lai and Daniel S. Morey, "Impact of Regime Type on the Influence of U.S. Foreign Aid," *Foreign Policy Analysis*, Vol. 2, No. 4, October 2006, pp. 385–404.

[77] Deborah A. Bräutigam and Stephen Knack, "Foreign Aid, Institutions, and Governance in Sub-Saharan Africa," *Economic Development and Cultural Change*, Vol. 52, No. 2, January 2004, p. 261.

[78] Bräutigam and Knack, 2004.

[79] Christopher Paul, Michael Nixon, Heather Peterson, Beth Grill, and Jessica Yeats, *The RAND Security Cooperation Prioritization and Propensity Matching Tool*, Santa Monica, Calif.: RAND Corporation, TL-112-OSD, 2013, p. 9.

[80] McNerney, O'Mahony, et al., 2014.

civil wars, terrorist attacks, and state repression.[81] More specifically, they evaluate the following four propositions derived from the aforementioned literature review:

1. U.S.-provided SSA has resulted in a net decrease (or increase) in the incidence of civil war and insurgency, terrorist attacks, and state repression in recipient states.
2. U.S.-provided SSA has been more effective in reducing political violence since the end of the Cold War than it was during the Cold War.
3. U.S.-provided SSA delivered in PKO contexts has been more effective than that delivered outside those contexts in reducing political violence.
4. U.S.-provided SSA has been more effective in reducing political violence in partner nations with good governance (i.e., those with higher-quality, more-robust state institutions and more-democratic politics) than in those without it.

Chapter Four briefly summarizes our research design, while Chapter Five presents our empirical findings.

---

[81] In Appendix C, we also conduct a deep dive on military coups. Although they are an important topic, and one that has recently received significant attention in some policy-making circles, the study of coups introduces several theoretical and conceptual challenges that necessitate a somewhat distinct empirical strategy from those used in the rest of our analysis. As such, we leave the analysis of coups to that appendix and encourage interested readers to refer to it for a deeper discussion.

CHAPTER FOUR

Research Approach for Evaluating the Impact That SSA Has in Africa

In this chapter, we describe the basic elements of our statistical models for testing the effectiveness of SSA in Africa. The chapter begins with a discussion of our outcomes of interest—civil wars, terrorism, and state repression—and the data used for each of them. Second, it explains how we incorporate the data on SSA described in Chapter Two into our statistical models. Third, it describes the various ways in which we account for the contexts in which SSA is implemented, including the effects of economic and political development, state bureaucratic and military capability, ethnic and societal opportunity, the geostrategic environment, ongoing and recent conflicts, and ongoing PKOs. Finally, it briefly explains our modeling strategy. We wrote this chapter for an audience not versed in statistical modeling; we attempted to use nontechnical language wherever possible. Readers interested in the technical details of our analysis should consult Appendix B, in which we provide extensive details on the construction of our models and tests of the robustness of our findings.

Measuring Intrastate Conflict

Our statistical models estimate SSA's effects on the incidence of intrastate conflict across African states since World War II. We rely more specifically on three measures of intrastate conflict: (1) civil-war onset, (2) terrorist attacks, and (3) levels of state repression. Taken together, these three measures provide us with a broad perspective on how levels of SSA affect multiple forms of conflict within African states. For each of these types of violence, we use data from social science data sets that are openly accessible, transparent in their construction, and widely used by academics and analysts in the policy community.

We drew data on civil-war onsets from the Armed Conflict Dataset from the Uppsala Conflict Data Program (UCDP)/Peace Research Institute Oslo (PRIO), which records whether each state is involved in a civil war in a given year.[1] Using these data, we measured whether a new period of civil war broke out in a given country and year.[2]

We measured terrorist attacks in two ways. First, using data from the Global Terrorism Database (GTD), we recorded the aggregate yearly number of terrorist attacks in each African state.[3] We did not distinguish between domestic and transnational terrorism, in part because the boundaries between these two types of violence are often indistinct and in part because SSA might be expected to either deter or disrupt and degrade all types of nonstate violent actors.[4] Second, we measured terrorist activity through the lethality of terrorist attacks, measured as the aggregate yearly number of casualties caused by terrorist attacks in each African state.

State repression is the use of violent or coercive actions by a government against its populace to retain power, maintain order, and

---

1 Nils Petter Gleditsch, Peter Wallensteen, Mikael Eriksson, Margareta Sollenberg, and Håvard Strand, "Armed Conflict 1946–2001: A New Dataset," *Journal of Peace Research*, Vol. 39, No. 5, 2002, pp. 615–637; Marie Allansson, Erik Melander, and Lotta Themnér, "Organized Violence, 1989–2016," *Journal of Peace Research*, Vol. 54, No. 4, 2017, pp. 574–587.

2 In our statistical models, we used two thresholds to measure the occurrence of conflicts and civil wars: 25 and 1,000 battle-related deaths, respectively. Related is that at least two years of peace must occur between conflicts for a new conflict to be measured as the start of a new period of civil war, rather than as a continuation of a previous conflict.

3 National Consortium for the Study of Terrorism and Responses to Terrorism, "Global Terrorism Database," last updated June 2017; Gary LaFree, Laura Dugan, and Erin Miller, *Putting Terrorism in Context: Lessons from the Global Terrorism Database*, Abingdon, Oxon: Routledge, 2015.

4 Walter Enders, Todd Sandler, and Khusrav Gaibulloev, "Domestic Versus Transnational Terrorism: Data, Decomposition, and Dynamics," *Journal of Peace Research*, Vol. 48, No. 3, 2011, pp. 319–337.

subdue political opponents through force.[5] Along those lines, we measured levels of state repression using the Cingranelli and Richards (CIRI) Human Rights Dataset, which measures the reported prevalence of governments' abuses of human rights along four dimensions—torture, political imprisonment, extrajudicial killings, and forced disappearances—based on annual reports compiled by Amnesty International and the U.S. State Department.[6] We then combined these four dimensions to form an aggregate index of state repression.

To test the robustness of our findings, we also analyzed several alternative measures of these three types of violence. We used different thresholds of violence for civil wars (the presence of government-sponsored militias as an alternative measure of possible repression). Although the focus of this chapter is on our primary measures of conflict, we also briefly discuss the results of our statistical models using these alternative measures in Appendix B.

Measuring SSA

We measured SSA in annual dollars for all countries and years between 1946 and 2015. Our main source for this information was the USAID Greenbook, which tracks the vast majority of all assistance provided to partner states.[7] We supplemented these data with additional information on several small and more-focused assistance programs specifically designed to bolster the security sectors of partner states and deter intrastate conflict. More specifically, we supplement the Greenbook data on levels of SSA with levels of 1206/2282 training and equipping funding, Section 1207 security and stabilization assistance, and funding via CTFP.[8]

---

5 Emily Hencken Ritter, "Policy Disputes, Political Survival, and the Onset and Severity of State Repression," *Journal of Conflict Resolution*, Vol. 58, No. 1, 2014, pp. 143–168.

6 David L. Cingranelli, David L. Richards, and K. Chad Clay, "The CIRI Human Rights Dataset," CIRI Human Rights Data Project, version 2014.04.14, April 4, 2014.

7 USAID, 2016.

8 Chapter Two provides further descriptive information on the distribution of U.S. SSA.

Levels of SSA vary significantly across states and over time, and, to account for these fluctuations and the differing characteristics of African states, we transformed the raw SSA data in several ways. In our models of civil war and terrorism, which are partly affected by interactions between the state and the populace, we scaled the magnitude of SSA by each state's population. In our models of state repression, which are affected by interactions between the government and military and by the quality of the state's military apparatus, we scaled the magnitude of SSA by the number of uniformed personnel in each state's military.

To account for any delays in reporting or between the provision and actual programming of SSA funding, we utilized a three-year moving average of SSA, which evened out any significant variation in yearly accounts of SSA funding and allowed us to assess the impact on more long-term trends in the amount of aid received by each state. Related is that, because we expect SSA's effects on mitigating intrastate violence to be somewhat delayed following implementation (per the discussion in Chapter Three), we utilized a four-year lag measure, meaning that our quantitative models assessed SSA's impact on intrastate conflict four years after aid is allocated.[9]

Controlling for Contextual Factors Affecting Intrastate Conflict and SSA

SSA is one of many factors that affect levels of intrastate conflict among African states. Furthermore, there are theoretical reasons to believe that SSA might be more or less effective in some states or conflict environments than in others.

To better isolate SSA's effects on levels of intrastate conflict from other structural characteristics of African states that might affect levels of violence, we also incorporated in our statistical models several other

[9] As discussed in greater detail in Appendix B, we also transformed the raw SSA data through the inverse hyperbolic sine transformation, which partly mitigated the effects of any outliers in our data.

factors associated with violent conflict. We briefly discuss those contextual factors here, with a more detailed description in Appendix B:

- **economic and political development:** Economic deprivation can foster resentment against incumbent governments. Conversely, wealthier states can more effectively provide welfare, security, and social services, and state wealth can proxy for more-capable governmental institutions, which should decrease states' risk of conflict.[10] Broadly representative and inclusive institutions can help resolve ideological differences and political disagreements through peaceful means, thus preventing conflict from erupting. Alternatively, particularly nondemocratic regimes might effectively utilize institutionalized repression to preemptively crush opposition before conflict or rely on force to degrade domestic challengers.[11]
- **natural-resource dependence:** Many African states are rich in lootable natural resources, and many states depend on the exploi-

10 Halvard Buhaug, Lars-Erik Cederman, and Kristian Skrede Gleditsch, "Square Pegs in Round Holes: Inequalities, Grievances, and Civil War," *International Studies Quarterly*, Vol. 58, No. 2, June 2014, pp. 418–431; Lars-Erik Cederman, Nils B. Weidmann, and Kristian Skrede Gleditsch, "Horizontal Inequalities and Ethnonationalist Civil War: A Global Comparison," *American Political Science Review*, Vol. 105, No. 3, August 2011, pp. 478–495; Paul Collier and Anke Hoeffler, "Greed and Grievance in Civil War," *Oxford Economic Papers*, Vol. 56, 2004, pp. 563–595; James D. Fearon and David D. Laitin, "Ethnicity, Insurgency, and Civil War," *American Political Science Review*, Vol. 97, No. 1, February 2003, pp. 75–90; Edward N. Muller, "Income Inequality, Regime Repressiveness, and Political Violence," *American Sociological Review*, Vol. 50, No. 1, February 1985, pp. 47–61; James A. Piazza, "Incubators of Terror: Do Failed and Failing States Promote Transnational Terrorism?" *International Studies Quarterly*, Vol. 52, No. 3, September 2008, pp. 469–488.

11 Deniz Aksoy, David B. Carter, and Joseph Wright, "Terrorism in Dictatorships," *Journal of Politics*, Vol. 74, No. 3, July 2012, pp. 810–826; Hanne Fjelde, "Generals, Dictators, and Kings: Authoritarian Regimes and Civil Conflict, 1973–2004," *Conflict Management and Peace Science*, Vol. 27, No. 3, 2010, pp. 185–218; Håvard Hegre, Tanja Ellingsen, Scott Gates, and Nils Petter Gleditsch, "Toward a Democratic Civil Peace? Democracy, Political Change, and Civil War, 1816–1992," *American Political Science Review*, Vol. 95, No. 1, March 2001, pp. 33–48; Matthew C. Wilson and James A. Piazza, "Autocracies and Terrorism: Conditioning Effects of Authoritarian Regime Type on Terrorist Attacks," *American Journal of Political Science*, Vol. 57, No. 4, October 2013, pp. 941–955.

tation of these resources to buoy their economies.[12] At the same time, natural resources present would-be militants and terrorists with both an attractive prize for successful conflict and the means to wage war against the state.[13] As such, a preponderance of natural-resource wealth should increase the risk that an African state would face internal challengers.

- **state bureaucratic and military capacity:** States with stronger bureaucracies should be able to both administratively deter violence through the more-efficient provision of public goods and make more-effective use of SSA.[14] Similarly, stronger, modernized, and more-coherent militaries should be able to broadly deter intrastate conflict by maintaining a preponderance of warfighting capabilities within the state.[15]
- **ethnic and societal opportunity:** Recent studies on intrastate conflict have documented the relationship between an increase in the size of a youth cohort and the onset of armed conflict and terrorist activity because younger populations provide a larger supply

---

[12] Navin A. Bapat and Sean Zeigler, "Terrorism, Dynamic Commitment Problems, and Military Conflict," *American Journal of Political Science*, Vol. 60, No. 2, April 2016, pp. 337–351.

[13] Päivi Lujala, "Deadly Combat over Natural Resources: Gems, Petroleum, Drugs, and the Severity of Armed Civil Conflict," *Journal of Conflict Resolution*, Vol. 53, No. 1, 2009, pp. 50–71; Päivi Lujala, "The Spoils of Nature: Armed Civil Conflict and Rebel Access to Natural Resources," *Journal of Peace Research*, Vol. 47, No. 1, 2010, pp. 15–28.

[14] Cullen S. Hendrix and Joseph K. Young, "State Capacity and Terrorism: A Two-Dimensional Approach," *Security Studies*, Vol. 23, No. 2, 2014, pp. 329–363.

[15] David E. Cunningham, Kristian Skrede Gleditsch, and Idean Salehyan, "It Takes Two: A Dyadic Analysis of Civil War Duration and Outcome," *Journal of Conflict Resolution*, Vol. 53, No. 4, August 2009, pp. 570–597; Gabriel Leon, "Loyalty for Sale? Military Spending and Coups d'État," *Public Choice*, Vol. 159, Nos. 3–4, June 2014, pp. 363–383; Ulrich Pilster and Tobias Böhmelt, "Coup-Proofing and Military Effectiveness in Interstate Wars, 1967–1999," *Conflict Management and Peace Science*, Vol. 28, No. 4, 2011, pp. 331–350; Jonathan M. Powell, "Determinants of the Attempting and Outcome of Coups d'État," *Journal of Conflict Resolution*, Vol. 56, No. 6, 2012, pp. 1017–1040; Jonathan M. Powell, "Trading Coups for Civil War: The Strategic Logic of Tolerating Rebellion," *African Security Review*, Vol. 23, No. 4, 2014, pp. 328–338.

of potential fighters.[16] A state might also be at an increased risk of intrastate conflict if a large portion of its population, particularly among ethnic minorities, is excluded from the state political apparatus. Political exclusion along ethnic lines enflames grievances against incumbent regimes, and widespread political exclusion challenges norms of popular representation. When excluded from political power, minority groups have few avenues other than armed resistance to redress these grievances.[17]

- **ongoing and recent intrastate conflicts:** Conflicts can spill over into nearby states, either through a direct expansion of conflict zones or indirectly through the transmission of weapons and revolutionary ideas. Related is that ongoing conflicts within the state can open opportunities for additional types of violence, either by increasing grievances among the populace or military or by making it easier to take up arms against the state, while past conflicts can leave conditions so bad that opportunities for conflict persist even after fighting ends.[18]

---

[16] Henrik Urdal, "A Clash of Generations? Youth Bulges and Political Violence," *International Studies Quarterly*, Vol. 50, No. 3, September 2006, pp. 607–629.

[17] Halvard Buhaug, Lars-Erik Cederman, and Jan Ketil Rød, "Disaggregating Ethno-Nationalist Civil Wars: A Dyadic Test of Exclusion Theory," *International Organization*, Vol. 62, No. 3, Summer 2008, pp. 531–551; Lars-Erik Cederman, Andreas Wimmer, and Brian Min, "Why Do Ethnic Groups Rebel? New Data and Analysis," *World Politics*, Vol. 62, No. 1, January 2010, pp. 87–119; Andreas Wimmer, Lars-Erik Cederman, and Brian Min, "Ethnic Politics and Armed Conflict: A Configurational Analysis of a New Global Data Set," *American Sociological Review*, Vol. 74, No. 2, 2009, pp. 316–337.

[18] Curtis Bell and Jun Koga Sudduth, "The Causes and Outcomes of Coup During Civil War," *Journal of Conflict Resolution*, Vol. 61, No. 7, 2017, pp. 1432–1455; Alex Braithwaite, "Resisting Infection: How State Capacity Conditions Conflict Contagion," *Journal of Peace Research*, Vol. 47, No. 3, 2010, pp. 311–319; Halvard Buhaug and Kristian Skrede Gleditsch, "Contagion or Confusion? Why Conflicts Cluster in Space," *International Studies Quarterly*, Vol. 52, No. 2, June 2008, pp. 215–233; Nathan Danneman and Emily Hencken Ritter, "Contagious Rebellion and Preemptive Repression," *Journal of Conflict Resolution*, Vol. 58, No. 2, 2014, pp. 254–279; Kristen A. Harkness, "The Ethnic Army and the State: Explaining Coup Traps and the Difficulties of Democratization in Africa," *Journal of Conflict Resolution*, Vol. 60, No. 4, 2016, pp. 587–616; John B. Londregan and Keith T. Poole, "Poverty, the Coup Trap, and the Seizure of Executive Power," *World Politics*, Vol. 42, No. 2, January 1990, pp. 151–183; Clayton Thyne, "The Impact of Coups d'État on Civil War Duration," *Conflict Management and Peace Science*, Vol. 34, No. 3, 2017, pp. 287–307; Barbara F.

- **geostrategic environment:** Although the primary threat to most African regimes comes from internal forms of conflict, such as insurgency and terrorism, external relations can greatly magnify these internal threats. Most importantly, the superpower competition of the Cold War era increased the likelihood of conflict through proxy wars. On the other hand, many governments in Africa could rely on support from former colonial powers. France, in particular, continued to play an active role on the continent long after decolonization.[19] Donor countries more generally have provided development assistance in part to reduce levels of violence and state fragility, particularly in the post–Cold War era.
- **PKOs:** As discussed in Chapter Three, ongoing PKOs are likely to influence SSA's success in mitigating intrastate conflict for at least two reasons. First, active PKOs are mechanisms of deep and repeated interactions between assisting states and their regional partners, which should promote greater oversight in how partner governments use SSA and greater cooperation among states in implementing SSA programs. Second, active PKOs suppress flare-ups in violence between warring parties in the state. Because we expect SSA to require sufficient time to yield positive change in the local security environment, having uniformed personnel maintain continued peace is likely valuable in providing a window for SSA to work in partner states.

All of these variables can influence the incidence of violence in Africa in either of two ways. First, they can exercise direct effects on the likelihood of conflict. Easily lootable natural resources, for instance, can provide both an incentive and the resources necessary for large-scale conflict, while militarily and bureaucratically strong regimes can deter would-be challengers. Second, they can influence the ways that the United States implements SSA itself. In the Cold War, for instance,

---

Walter, "Does Conflict Beget Conflict? Explaining Recurring Civil War," *Journal of Peace Research*, Vol. 41, No. 3, 2004, pp. 371–388.

[19] Christopher S. Clapham, *Africa and the International System: The Politics of State Survival*, New York: Cambridge University Press, 1996.

the United States' primary goal was to prevent the alignment of African partner nations with the Soviet Union, and the United States was willing to downplay governance concerns as a result. During ongoing PKOs, the United States enjoys much greater oversight and leverage when attempting to foster change in partner security institutions through SSA.

To account for the direct effects of these various factors, we were able to include control variables for each of them in our statistical models. To account for the ways in which they influence the actual implementation of SSA, however, we needed to rely on interaction terms and period effects. In line with these expectations, we specified quantitative models that (1) bifurcated the analysis between the Cold War and post–Cold War periods, (2) interacted levels of SSA with a dichotomous indicator for the presence of an ongoing UN PKO at the time of SSA implementation, and (3) interacted levels of SSA with different measures of partner-nation governance.

Not all of these factors are relevant for every outcome, however. Consequently, we included only those variables that were appropriate for the specific outcome we were trying to predict. Table 4.1 summarizes the variables included in our models for each type of political violence.

Modeling Approaches and Selection Effects

Having described the data and our measures of SSA, we now discuss our modeling approach. We conducted a quantitative analysis that combines all African countries (excluding Egypt) in the post–World War II period. The unit of analysis is the country-year. A country-year (e.g., Morocco-2005) uniquely identifies a specific country for a particular year. For any given outcome measure, our quantitative models estimated SSA's effects while controlling for a variety of confounding factors. We used different methods depending on the outcome of interest: logistical regression for binary variables, such as civil-war onset; ordinary least squares (OLS) regression for the continuous measure we

Table 4.1
Control and Conditioning Variables to Isolate the Effects That SSA Has on Intrastate Conflict

Variable	Civil War	Terrorist Attacks	State Repression
GDP per capita	x	x	x
Level of democracy (polity level)	x	x	
Military regime			x
Personalist regime			x
Single-party regime			x
Democracy			x
Military spending per service member	x	x	
State bureaucratic capacity		x	
Excluded-population size	x	x	
Youth bulge	x	x	
Neighborhood civil war	x		
Ongoing civil war		x	x
Previous civil war	x		
Previous coup attempt	x		
Percentage of GDP from natural-resource rents	x		
Ongoing PKO	x	x	x
Development assistance	x	x	x
Arms transfers from Russia or China	x		
Cold War	x	x	x
Francophone Africa	x	x	x

NOTE: GDP = gross domestic product.

employed for state repression; or a negative binomial model for terrorist attacks.

Our models include only those country-years for which we have sufficient data on key variables.[20] Depending on the precise model, the number of country-years can range from 326 to 1,635, with most models of the full time period (1946 to 2015) having more than 1,000 observations and those for the Cold War and post–Cold War periods often having 700 or more. This relatively sizable sample allowed us to identify several broad patterns. As the propositions we tested became more nuanced, however (such as evaluating SSA's effects during ongoing PKOs in the post–Cold War era), the number of observations—and thus our ability to reliably discern statistical regularities—declined.

Unfortunately, identifying the effects of SSA is complicated by a selection problem. Observational studies of conflict are often plagued by selection problems, and we have good reason to suspect this problem in the case of SSA. The selection problem results from the basic process that makes some countries more or less likely to receive SSA in the first place. SSA is not randomly allocated. Instead, policymakers deliberately select partner states, allocating aid based on a variety of strategic interests and political and economic conditions. To the extent that these same factors associate with civil war or a poor human-rights record, we had to worry that any relationship we detected might be inflated or entirely driven by selection. If U.S. aid disproportionately flows to conflict regions, it might appear that SSA causes conflict when, in fact, the relationship might be the reverse. Conversely, if U.S. aid flows to stable, capable partners, our analysis would overstate the beneficial effects of SSA if we failed to control for this selection.

Scholars have long recognized this concern and offer a variety of potential solutions.[21] All of them share a basic approach: Given that

---

[20] We also ran variants of our models with imputed data to attempt to restore the statistical power lost through missing data. Unfortunately, data imputation poses its own problems, so we used models with imputed data only as robustness checks.

[21] Steven C. Poe and James Meernik, "US Military Aid in the 1980s: A Global Analysis," *Journal of Peace Research*, Vol. 32, No. 4, 1995, pp. 399–411; James Meernik, Eric L. Krueger, and Steven C. Poe, "Testing Models of U.S. Foreign Policy: Foreign Aid During and After the Cold War," *Journal of Politics*, Vol. 60, No. 1, February 1998, pp. 63–85;

we know that SSA recipients are not randomly selected, we can model this selection process (albeit imperfectly) and incorporate it into our analysis. In effect, this approach begins by trying to answer the question of why some countries (in some years) receive SSA and others do not. If we could first describe the strategic logic of this policy choice, we would then be able to model it. This approach is often called *two-stage modeling*.

In the first stage, we modeled the conditions that make states more likely to receive SSA. We used the results from this analysis to create propensity weights, which represented each country's likelihood of receiving SSA in any given year. We then included these weights in the second stage, which modeled SSA's effects on civil war, terrorism, or any other outcome of interest. These propensity weights could rebalance the data to correct for selection, but they were not a perfect fix. Their value crucially depended on data quality and availability. We can model only observable factors that drove the selection process. Our propensity weights will be imperfect to the extent that selection derived from unobservable or poorly measured factors.

Notwithstanding these challenges, we believed that propensity weighting could reduce selection bias and increase our overall confidence in the results. As a result, we incorporated these weights in all of our quantitative models.

Having generally described our empirical strategy, we now turn to the results. Readers who wish to learn the full technical details of our data and models can find them in Appendix A and Appendix B.

Shannon Lindsey Blanton, "Promoting Human Rights and Democracy in the Developing World: U.S. Rhetoric Versus U.S. Arms Exports," *American Journal of Political Science*, Vol. 44, No. 1, January 2000, pp. 123–131; Shannon Lindsey Blanton, "Foreign Policy in Transition? Human Rights, Democracy, and U.S. Arms Exports," *International Studies Quarterly*, Vol. 49, No. 4, December 2005, pp. 647–667; Andrew Boutton and David B. Carter, "Fair-Weather Allies? Terrorism and the Allocation of US Foreign Aid," *Journal of Conflict Resolution*, Vol. 58, No. 7, 2014, pp. 1144–1173.

CHAPTER FIVE
Findings on the Impact That SSA Has in Africa

As described in Chapter Four, we modeled SSA's effects in two stages, first determining where the United States provides SSA and then evaluating its effects in those countries. In this chapter, we first review the types of countries that typically receive more or less aid. In the rest of the chapter, we discuss SSA's effects on civil wars, terrorism, and state repression, in turn.

We wrote this chapter for a general audience, using nontechnical language and presentation of statistical results wherever possible. Readers who want to know the details of our model specifications, data sources (and limitations), precise statistical results, and tests for robustness can find all of this information in Appendix B.

Recipients of SSA: First-Stage Models

In its simplest form, our study asked, "What is SSA's effect on political violence?" But before we could address this question, we needed to account for the selection process that determines which states receive SSA. Our first-stage models evaluate the factors that drive this strategic choice. As the time-serial plots in Chapter Two illustrated, the number of recipients has changed over time. In this chapter, we delve deeper into this change and consider how SSA allocation varies between the Cold War and post–Cold War periods.

Table 5.1 summarizes the relationship between different characteristics of U.S. partner nations and the international environment on the one hand and, on the other, the likelihood that the United States

Table 5.1
Summary of Factors Affecting the Likelihood That a Country Will Receive SSA

Factor	All Years	Cold War	Post–Cold War
Political and economic development			
Level of democracy (polity level)			
Political corruption			
State repression			
GDP per capita			
Domestic security and recent conflict			
Youth bulge			
Political instability			
Neighborhood civil war			
Time since last successful coup			
Time since last civil war			
International conflict environment			
Arms transfers from Russia or China			
Post-9/11			
Cold War			
Soviet ally			
Observations	2,171	1,148	1,023

NOTE: Color indicates the direction of the relationship, if any: Green indicates a statistically significant increase in the likelihood of receiving SSA, red indicates a statistically significant decrease, and no color indicates no statistically significant change to the likelihood of receiving aid. Shading indicates the degree of statistical significance: Darker indicates a higher level of statistical significance.

will allocate assistance.[1] We have color-coded the results to represent the direction of the relationship, while the shading indicates the degree of statistical significance. Green cells indicate those factors associated with a statistically significantly higher likelihood of SSA in our model, while red cells indicate those factors associated with a statistically significantly lower likelihood. The darker shading indicates a more robust statistical relationship.

First, consider how regime characteristics and other political conditions of a partner nation shape this selection choice. Generally, we find that such conditions operated in significantly different ways across the Cold War and post–Cold War periods. During the Cold War, more-corrupt and more-autocratic states were more likely than their counterparts to receive SSA. Neither of these effects, however, appears in the post–Cold War period. Rather, for the post–Cold War period, we find that less repressive states were more likely to receive SSA. No such result holds for the Cold War period. These results suggest that, during the Cold War, U.S. policymakers were far less concerned than they are today about providing SSA to corrupt and undemocratic regimes. And their choices of recipients were unrelated to a partner nation's level of human-rights abuses or other forms of repression.

We also see that, beyond regime characteristics, domestic security conditions partly drive the choices of SSA recipients. There is some weak evidence that, during the Cold War, countries that recently experienced some political change (i.e., toward higher or lower levels of democracy) were more likely than those that had not experienced such change to receive SSA. We can also see this concern about domestic instability in the strongly positive relationship between SSA and a country experiencing a youth bulge (i.e., large shocks of young, fighting-age men). At the same time, however, we find that, during the Cold War, the United States preferred partner nations that had not recently experienced civil wars or coups. As a country gets further

---

[1] In our primary models, for us to consider a partner nation "selected" for U.S. SSA, it had to receive at least \$1 million (in constant U.S. dollars) in a given year. This threshold is extremely low but eliminated those countries that receive only token amounts of assistance. In alternative models, we set the threshold to \$10 million in a given year; the results largely remained the same with the higher threshold. Details can be found in Appendix B.

in time since its last civil war or coup, it is more likely to receive SSA. Such a finding might suggest that, during the Cold War, the United States preferred more-stable countries as SSA recipients. There is no evidence of a similar trend in the post–Cold War period.

Finally, we include several variables meant to capture the broader strategic or international environment. In general, we find that countries were less likely to receive SSA in the Cold War period. As discussed in Chapter Two, this finding is likely driven by the early Cold War years (e.g., the 1960s and 1970s), when less than 30 percent of countries received any aid in a typical year. As Figure 2.3 in that chapter showed, the number of recipients dramatically increased in the 1980s, and it has remained high throughout the post–Cold War period. After controlling for other variables, we see no significant difference in the post-9/11 period. Other, more-nuanced measures of strategic interests also shed light on the varying selection process over time. As expected, Soviet allies were far less likely than other countries to receive SSA. That being said, the measure of adversary arms transfers produces surprising results. Consistent with the result on Soviet allies is our finding that these arms transfers made it less likely that a state had received SSA during the Cold War. However, adversary arms transfers were positively associated with receiving SSA in the post–Cold War period. This result might suggest a new competitive pressure driving SSA provision in Africa. With the distinction between allied and enemy states less stark after the Cold War, the United States might use SSA to compete for influence in countries that Russia and China have traditionally controlled or are actively pursuing.

Civil War

As discussed in Chapter Three, SSA, if implemented effectively, should ideally make the security forces of partner states stronger and more capable. Stronger security forces, in turn, should lower partner states' risk of civil war, either by deterring potential insurgents from taking up arms or by suppressing insurgent forces more quickly. By the same logic, larger levels of SSA, by providing for greater improvements in partner states' security structures, should decrease the risk of civil war more than small amounts of aid would. On the other hand, there are reasons that SSA might have counterproductive effects. It might make partner governments more willing to rely on violent repression rather than peaceful cooptation of opposition, increasing popular grievances, and, in turn, levels of rebellion against the state.[2] Alternatively, it might touch off interethnic security dilemmas that cause ethnic groups that are not represented in the government or security services to develop their own militias in a (real or perceived) need for self-defense.[3]

Table 5.2 summarizes the relationship in our statistical models between SSA (and contextual variables) and states' risk of civil war.[4]

Table 5.2
The Effects That SSA Has on the Risk of Civil War Among African States

	Models for SSA			Models for SSA with PKOs	
Factor	**All Years**	**Cold War**	**Post–Cold War**	**All Years**	**Post–Cold War**
SSA					
SSA					
SSA with ongoing PKO	n/a	n/a	n/a		
Controls					
PKO, one-year lag[a]					
PKO, four-year lag					
GDP per capita					
Polity level					
Polity level, squared					

2 Fjelde, 2010.

3 Buhaug, Cederman, and Rød, 2008; Cederman, Wimmer, and Min, 2010; Posen, 1993; Wimmer, Cederman, and Min, 2009.

4 The relationships summarized in Table 5.2 reference our statistical models using a threshold of 25 battle-related deaths to mark the onset of civil war. Appendix B also provides analyses using a threshold of 1,000 battle-related deaths to mark the onset of civil war.

Table 5.2—Continued

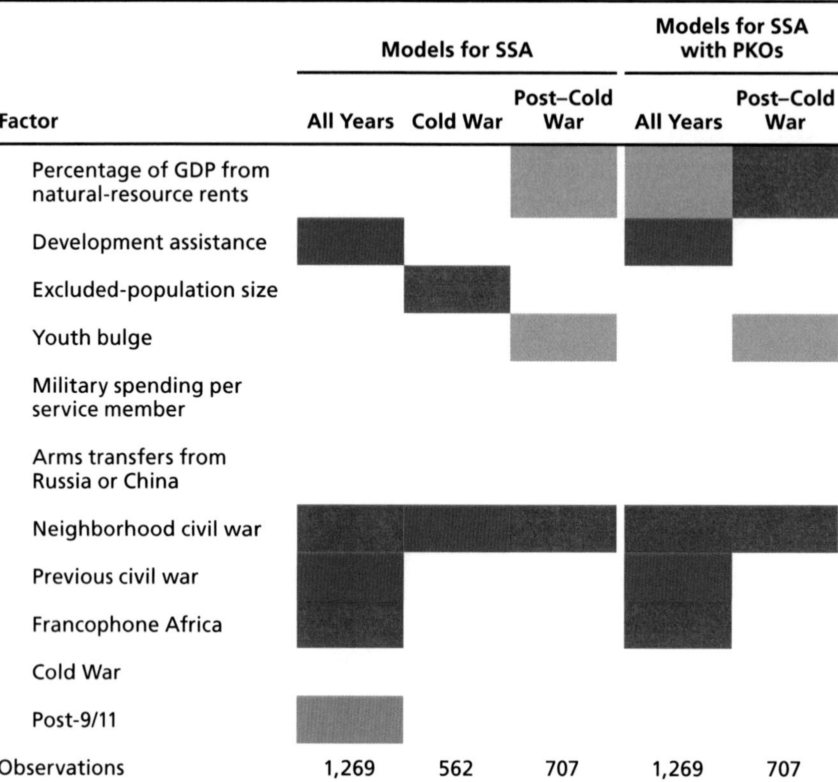

Factor	Models for SSA			Models for SSA with PKOs	
	All Years	Cold War	Post–Cold War	All Years	Post–Cold War
Percentage of GDP from natural-resource rents					
Development assistance					
Excluded-population size					
Youth bulge					
Military spending per service member					
Arms transfers from Russia or China					
Neighborhood civil war					
Previous civil war					
Francophone Africa					
Cold War					
Post-9/11					
Observations	1,269	562	707	1,269	707

NOTE: To mark the onset of civil war, each model uses a threshold of 25 battle-related deaths. Color-coding indicates the direction of the relationship, if any: Green indicates a statistically significant decrease in states' risk of civil war, red indicates a statistically significant increase in states' risk of civil war, and no color indicates no statistically significant change to civil-war risk in our statistical models. Shading indicates the degree of statistical significance: Darker indicates a higher level of statistical significance. n/a = not applicable.

[a] *Lag* refers to amount of time after aid was allocated that our quantitative models assess SSA's impact on intrastate conflict.

Green cells indicate factors associated with a statistically significant decrease in states' risk of civil war, while red cells indicate factors associated with a statistically significant increase in states' risk of civil war.

When looking at the full period from the end of World War II to the present, we find that increasing levels of SSA significantly increase the risk of civil war among African states. That is, according to our statistical models, partner states are more likely to experience a civil war in the years following the provision of SSA, and this risk increases further as greater levels of aid are provided.

Further analyses reveal, however, that this adverse relationship between SSA and civil war was largely contained to the Cold War period.[5] For the Cold War period, increasing levels of SSA were associated with an increased risk of civil war in our models.[6] During the post–Cold War period, however, we found no statistically significant relationship between levels of SSA and states' risk of experiencing civil war, meaning that SSA neither significantly increased nor significantly decreased states' risk of conflict.[7]

The absence of an overall relationship between U.S.-provided SSA and civil wars in the post–Cold War era does not necessarily mean that there is no effect. As discussed in Chapter Three, U.S. assistance could potentially either reduce or incite civil wars. SSA might have both effects (positive and negative) in different countries at various times, depending on the context and the amounts and types of U.S. assistance provided. Our analysis simply suggests that there has been no net reduction (or increase) in wars across the continent as a result of U.S. assistance in the post–Cold War period. Although our analyses of SSA in different subsets of contexts did not find any robust relationships between SSA and civil wars (as described in more detail in Appendix B), an analysis of different types of SSA (or SSA implemented in different ways) might find different effects, depending on context. As we discuss in Chapter Six, this distinction is important. If certain types

---

[5] For reference, there were slightly fewer civil-war onsets among African states during the Cold War than during the post–Cold War period, with 35 civil wars beginning during the Cold War period and 41 civil wars beginning during the post–Cold War period.

[6] This relationship was statistically significant in our baseline models, albeit at a relatively low threshold of statistical significance. In alternative models using a range of lags, the relationship did not quite reach these thresholds, although they were usually close. Appendix B provides full details.

[7] To better understand these diverging effects, Figure B.2 in Appendix B plots the predicted risk of civil war over the range of SSA levels in our analyses in the Cold War and post–Cold War periods, respectively.

of U.S. SSA are having different impacts depending on context, the United States must better employ risk analysis to identify contexts in which SSA is having counterproductive effects. Alternatively, certain low-cost SSA programs might be effective (or potentially counterproductive), while the larger-budget ones are not. If this were the case, the effects of the low-cost programs might not be discernible statistically when grouped together with the much larger, less effective programs. If this latter dynamic accounts for our results, it suggests at a minimum that U.S. SSA is highly inefficient and funds should be reallocated to programs that show rigorous evidence of effectiveness.

The divergent effects of SSA in the Cold War and post–Cold War periods are likely explained by two factors. First, during the Cold War, the United States was more interested in ensuring that partners in Africa retained their alignment with the United States than with questions of good governance by partner states. By focusing on great power balancing, rather than partners' domestic stability and governance, the United States might have maintained its influence on the continent but only by contributing to domestic political instability (e.g., by emboldening the partner government to act repressively). In contrast, in the post–Cold War era, the United States has been principally concerned with the consequences of domestic instability—humanitarian suffering, refugee flows, the potential for spillover violence, and eventually (after the September 11 terrorist attacks) with terrorism. It therefore structured its SSA allocations to try to reduce the risk of civil war on the continent.

Second, because the United States and the Soviet Union were locked in a competition for influence, any move by one superpower was likely to be countered by the other. Consequently, U.S. assistance to a country in Africa might have increased the likelihood that the Soviet Union would provide assistance to that country's dissidents, which frequently results in proxy wars.

History provides numerous examples of exactly these dynamics. During the Angolan civil war in the 1970s, the United States provided military aid to the National Union for the Total Independence of Angola (União Nacional para a Independência Total de Angola, or UNITA) in the 1970s, which was countered by Soviet and Cuban support to the rival Popular Movement for the Liberation of Angola.[8] The United States and the Soviet Union backed different factions in the DRC over several decades; this included U.S. support for the military-backed Mobuto regime against Soviet-supported rebels in the 1970s and 1980s.[9]

We investigated other ways besides the effects of the Cold War in which context might influence how SSA was conducted. More specifically, we assessed whether SSA was more effective among certain types of partners than others, and we evaluated whether the effects of SSA conducted in conjunction with an ongoing PKO differed from those of SSA distributed in ordinary environments.

Surprisingly, we found no statistically significant differences in SSA's effects between different types of partner states.[10] As Chapter Two discussed, previous research has found that SSA was particularly effective among states with "good governance"—that is, those states with more-effective bureaucracies and more-democratic politics. Given the weakness of many states throughout Africa, our indicators might simply not have had enough variation for the effects of governance to be apparent. That is, when we compare an extremely weak state, such as CAR, with a highly effective state, such as the Republic of Korea, differences in SSA effectiveness might be readily apparent, while they are much less apparent when the comparison is between CAR and Zambia or Tanzania.

When we examined SSA's effects in the presence of PKOs, however, we found very different patterns. As discussed in Chapter Three, PKOs provide a very different context for SSA. Interactions between international and local government officials are much more common, providing more opportunities for both socialization and oversight. Certain mechanisms provide greater coordination and continuity over time in the approach of the international community. The interna-

8 U.S. Department of State, undated (b).

9 Metz, 1996; U.S. Department of State, "Global Security Contingency Fund (GSCF)," undated (a).

10 See Appendix B for a more detailed discussion of SSA's effects in the context of different types of partner states.

tional community also enjoys much greater leverage over the partner nation because of the resources being committed. At the same time, international peacekeepers provide reassurance to the various communities in the host state, opening up a period of time in which reforms can take root without the same risks that other fragile states encounter. SSA, in short, can be implemented more in line with the prescriptions of the SSR paradigm.

In line with the expectations of the SSR literature is our finding that SSA implemented in conjunction with an ongoing PKO reduces the likelihood of renewed civil conflict—even after accounting for the independent effects of ongoing PKOs.[11] It is important to note, however, that, although it is statistically significant and substantively meaningful for the broader SSR literature, our finding of these effects is based on a relatively small sample size of PKOs, meaning that the results of our models are not necessarily robust or generalizable to different contexts. Liberia—a case generally regarded as a success story—accounts for a substantial portion of the positive relationship. Other cases in which the United States provided at least $1 million in SSA to a country hosting a postconflict PKO include Cote d'Ivoire, the DRC, Mozambique, and Sierra Leone. Of these, all but the DRC are generally considered successes. In the cases of Cote d'Ivoire and Sierra Leone, however, France and the United Kingdom, respectively, were the major international actors (aside from the UN). Because we cannot directly measure SSA provided by U.S. allies, such as the United Kingdom and France, we cannot determine how much of the positive outcomes derived from U.S. assistance rather than that of allies. In all, these significant results suggest that the combination of PKOs and SSA does yield meaningful impacts in partner states, but additional analyses should be conducted to further substantiate and refine these findings.

Finally, the contextual variables that control for other factors affecting the risk of civil war in Table 5.2 also provide some potentially useful insights. However, we should be cautious when interpreting these findings. We designed our quantitative models to evaluate SSA's

---

[11] Figure B.3 in Appendix B provides a visual representation of SSA's substantive effects in states with active PKOs, as predicted by our statistical models.

effects of on civil-war onset; as a result, they might not serve as a proper test of these other contextual factors. Notwithstanding this caveat, we find that the results are largely consistent with expectations from prior work. Wealthier countries, as seen in the results for GDP per capita, are less likely to experience a civil war. This trend holds except for resource-rich (e.g., oil-producing) states, which are significantly more likely to suffer from civil wars. We also find that civil wars tend to be more likely when a neighboring state is engulfed in civil war, capturing potential spillover or contagion effects. Surprisingly, this last result is highly significant across all models except during the Cold War, when the relationship reverses but is only marginally significant.

Terrorism

In much the same way that SSA should deter civil war by strengthening partner states' security forces and minimizing opportunities for violence, it should also decrease levels of terrorist activity in partner states. Stronger security forces can more capably degrade and dismantle terrorist networks within their borders, and stronger security structures should deter more would-be terrorists from violence.[12]

Table 5.3 summarizes the relationship between SSA and the annual number of terrorist attacks.[13] Green indicates a statistically significant decrease in the annual number of terrorist attacks in African states. Conversely, red indicates a statistically significant increase in the annual number of terrorist attacks in African states.

Increasing levels of SSA to African states neither significantly increased nor decreased levels of terrorist activity across all countries

[12] Because more-capable security forces should be able to suppress all types of terrorism, our main statistical models of terrorist activity do not distinguish between acts of domestic and transnational terrorism. However, we also present alternative models that separate SSA's effects on levels of domestic and transnational terrorism, respectively, in Appendix B. Our substantive conclusions remain the same.

[13] The results are qualitatively the same when we instead use annual number of casualties from terrorist attacks as our outcome measure. In Appendix B, we discuss those results in greater detail.

Table 5.3
The Effects That SSA Has on the Number of Terrorist Attacks in African States

	Models for SSA			Models for SSA with PKOs	
Factor	**All Years**	**Cold War**	**Post–Cold War**	**All Years**	**Post–Cold War**
SSA					
SSA					
SSA with ongoing PKO	n/a	n/a	n/a		
Controls					
PKO, with one-year lag					
PKO, with four-year lag					
GDP per capita					
Polity level					
Polity level, squared					
State bureaucratic capacity					
Development assistance					
Excluded-population size					
Youth bulge					
Military spending per service member					
Ongoing civil war					
Francophone Africa					
Cold War					
Post-9/11					
Attacks in previous year					
Observations	1,635	719	916	1,635	916

Table 5.3—Continued

Factor	Models for SSA			Models for SSA with PKOs	
	All Years	Cold War	Post–Cold War	All Years	Post–Cold War

NOTE: Color-coding indicates the direction of the relationship, if any: Green indicates a statistically significant decrease in the annual number of terrorist attacks in African states, red indicates a statistically significant increase in the number, and no color indicates no statistically significant change. Shading indicates the degree of statistical significance: Darker indicates a higher level of statistical significance.

in our models. This relationship, or lack thereof, persists in both the Cold War and post–Cold War periods. Additionally, our models found no robust evidence that the effects of SSA are significantly different among different types of partner states.[14]

As in the case of civil wars in the post–Cold War era, the absence of a net effect of U.S.-provided SSA on terrorist activity across the continent does not necessarily mean that there is no effect in each specific case. Again, we looked for more–context-contingent effects using a variety of tests, although data quality limited the range of analyses we could undertake. With improved data on different types of SSA in specific countries, more-nuanced relationships might be identifiable.

The one exception that we were able to identify again concerns the effects of PKOs. As in our analysis of civil wars, we expect that, because of deeper interactions and added physical barriers to violence, SSA should have a greater effect in mitigating terrorist activity when a PKO is also present in the partner state. In line with these expectations is our finding that increasing levels of SSA significantly decreases levels of terrorist activity in states with active PKOs, both in the numbers of terrorist attacks and in the numbers of casualties caused by terrorist attacks.[15] In contrast, SSA provided to states without active PKOs had no statistically significant effect on levels of terrorist activity.

---

[14] See Appendix B for a more detailed discussion of SSA's effects on terrorist activity in the context of different types of partner states.

[15] Like in our civil-war models, these statistically significant relationships are found in both the post–Cold War era and in the entire post–World War II era. However, because most

It is important to note that terrorist activity is generally low in countries with UN PKOs. Consequently, even though U.S.-provided SSA has a proportionally very large effect, the absolute decline in terrorist attacks and fatalities is low (from just less than two predicted attacks per year in the absence of SSA to effectively zero when the United States provides substantial amounts of assistance). In conjunction with our other results, however, the decline provides further indication that SSA is having its intended effects when implemented in a conducive environment. More specifically, it suggests that SSA must be paired with increased coordination and mechanisms of improved oversight into how SSA is implemented to see desired reductions in terrorist activity among partner states. These findings are consistent with calls for the United States and other SSA providers to increase oversight of SSA programs and to ensure that SSA contributes to institutional reform.[16]

The contextual variables in Table 5.3 reveal several trends in terrorist activity in Africa. As with civil wars, we find that wealthier countries tend to be better off, experiencing fewer terrorist attacks, particularly during the post–Cold War period. Although this relationship is not quite as strong as it was for civil wars, we see a much more significant role for official development assistance (ODA), which strongly associates with a decrease in terrorist activity. ODA appears to have a positive effect in every model except the Cold War period. Unsurprisingly, we find that terrorist activity increases significantly during civil wars and that states experiencing more terrorist attacks in previous years are more likely to experience greater levels of attacks in sub-

---

PKOs have occurred in the post–Cold War era, we constrain our discussion to this period. To help visualize these effects further, Appendix B provides plots of the predicted number of terrorist attacks over a range of SSA allocations to partner states.

[16] Jon Temin, "Somalia and the Limits of U.S. Bombing," *New York Times*, May 25, 2017; UN Security Council, "Despite Progress Since Peace Accord, Mali Still Needs International Support to Face Accelerating Challenges, Peacekeeping Chief Tells Security Council," 7,917th meeting, SC/12779, April 6, 2017; Baker, 2016.

sequent years.[17] This association is our most robust result among our control variables, remaining highly significant across all models and time periods.[18]

State Repression

States commonly turn to violent repression to circumvent deficiencies in the capabilities of their security forces. That is, weaker states often utilize violent repression to prop up their regimes as a preemptive measure against domestic opposition forces. SSA, by improving the capabilities of partner states' security forces, then, might decrease levels of violent repression by partner militaries and gradually steer partner states toward greater respect for human rights. Alternatively, states with highly capable security forces might feel no need to co-opt opposition, instead repressing any expressions of discontent with the existing political order.

In states without PKOs, SSA appears to have no net effect, positive or negative, in either the Cold War or post–Cold War period. Table 5.4 summarizes the relationship between SSA and levels of state repression in our statistical models. Green indicates a statistically significant decrease in levels of state repression among African states. Conversely, red indicates a statistically significant increase in levels of state repression among African states.

Again, this finding does not rule out the possibility that certain types of SSA are having opposite effects in different contexts. It is nonetheless significant that SSA as a whole does not seem to have

---

[17] To account for possible statistical bias by including lags of the previous year's terrorist attacks, we also present alternative statistical models in Appendix B in which we do not account for terrorist attacks in previous years.

[18] Michael J. Findley and Joseph K. Young, "More Combatant Groups, More Terror? Empirical Tests of an Outbidding Logic," *Terrorism and Political Violence*, Vol. 24, No. 5, November 2012b, pp. 706–721; Michael J. Findley and Joseph K. Young, "Terrorism and Civil War: A Spatial and Temporal Approach to a Conceptual Problem," *Perspectives on Politics*, Vol. 10, No. 2, June 2012a, pp. 285–305; Virginia Page Fortna, "Do Terrorists Win? Rebels' Use of Terrorism and Civil War Outcomes," *International Organization*, Vol. 69, No. 3, Summer 2015, pp. 519–556.

Table 5.4
The Effects That SSA Has on State Repression in African States

	Models for SSA			Models for SSA with PKOs	
Factor	**All Years**	**Cold War**	**Post–Cold War**	**All Years**	**Post–Cold War**
SSA					
SSA					
SSA with ongoing PKO	n/a	n/a	n/a		
Controls					
PKO, with one-year lag					
PKO, with four-year lag					
GDP per capita					
Level of democracy (polity level)					
Military regime					
Personalist regime					
Single-party regime					
Development assistance					
Ongoing civil war					
Francophone Africa					
Cold War					
Post-9/11					
Repression in previous year					
Observations	1,260	326	934	1,260	934

NOTE: Color-coding indicates the direction of the relationship, if any: Green indicates a statistically significant decrease in levels of state repression used by African governments, red indicates a statistically significant increase, and no color indicates no statistically significant change. Shading indicates the degree of statistical significance: Darker indicates a higher level of statistical significance.

contributed to improved observance of human rights, even in the post–Cold War era, in which Leahy vetting, E-IMET, and other programs and practices have sought to improve the human-rights contributions of SSA. On the other hand, the absence of an overall relationship contradicts the claims of critics of U.S. assistance, who have frequently argued that the "war on terror" has had widespread pernicious effects on human-rights practices in Africa.

Once again, however, among states with active PKOs at the time of assistance, U.S. SSA appears to have beneficial effects.[19] The divergent outcomes in ordinary environments and those in which peacekeepers are deployed suggest that, to be effective and achieve its intended results, SSA must be paired with additional mechanisms that foster close cooperation and increased oversight.

The contextual variables in Table 5.4 suggest a story remarkably consistent with that of civil wars and terrorist activity. Increasing levels of wealth and development assistance are associated with lower levels of state repression. ODA is similarly associated with lower levels of state repression. The latter result almost certainly reflects some degree of selection bias, with more-repressive states losing out on ODA, but the overall trend is consistent with our previous findings for these factors. And like with terrorist activity, we find that an ongoing civil war is associated with an increase in state repression. These models also include measures that capture different types of authoritarian regimes, which also reveal potential variation in state repression. Compared with single-party autocracies, we find, personalist dictatorships and military regimes are generally more repressive. Although this association is especially significant for military regimes, neither result holds for the Cold War period. That being said, because of missing data on state repression, we have very few observations in the Cold War model and should be especially careful when interpreting this result.

---

[19] Like in our previous models, these statistically significant relationships are found in both the post–Cold War era and in the entire post–World War II era. However, because most PKOs have occurred in the post–Cold War era, we constrain our discussion to this period.

Conclusion

Over the course of this chapter, we have empirically explored the various ways in which SSA might affect civil conflict and other violent outcomes in Africa. A full evaluation of SSA's effects must account for the differential impact across time and context for each of these outcomes. Having already discussed our specific results for civil wars, terrorism, and repression, we now take a step back to consider the broader findings for SSA.

Overall, we have found that SSA has not only been allocated differently across the Cold War and post–Cold War periods—with a greater focus on less corrupt, less repressive, and more-democratic countries in the latter period—but its effects have also varied significantly. For the Cold War period, total SSA is associated with an increased risk of civil war. We found no robust results of SSA's overall effects in the post–Cold War period. However, SSA in the presence of a PKO appears to work in a positive direction: It is associated with less risk of civil war, terrorist activity, and repression. These findings further reveal the importance of context in understanding the effects of SSA.

CHAPTER SIX

Conclusions and Policy Recommendations

Summary and Discussion of Findings

The statistical analyses detailed in this report allow us to discern broad trends with important implications both for policy and for future evaluations of SSA.

The United States Deemphasized Governance Issues During Cold War Competition

SSA appears to have been allocated very differently in the Cold War and post–Cold War periods. During the Cold War, the United States' primary goal was to maintain partnerships with governments in Africa and to prevent regimes from slipping into the Soviet orbit. Enhancing governance or human rights—or even maintaining peace and stability—were not the overriding goals of U.S. assistance in this period. Consistent with this reading of U.S. foreign policy is our finding that the United States was more likely to provide SSA to more-autocratic and more-corrupt governments in this period while, unsurprisingly, steering aid away from Soviet allies and partners. In the post–Cold War era, in contrast, the United States provided less aid to repressive governments. It also tended to prioritize countries recovering from civil wars. These findings are consistent with numerous studies that have found that U.S. development assistance also changed considerably in the post–Cold War era.

From a methodological perspective, the differences between the two periods highlight the importance of isolating SSA's impact in each of these two periods. Many statistical analyses of SSA examine the two eras together, attempting to isolate the effects of the Cold War with a control variable for the years up to 1989 or 1991. Such an approach would be adequate if the Cold War had not affected the way in which SSA itself was allocated or implemented. But if the modalities of SSA itself changed from one period to the next, a simple control variable is not adequate. This difference in modeling approaches influences the conclusions that various analysts draw. In broad terms, previous analyses that have used more data from the Cold War period have generally come to more-pessimistic conclusions about the effects of U.S.-provided SSA, while those that drew more data from the post–Cold War era have generally been more optimistic.[1] The results of our first-stage models that predicted where the United States directed SSA can help to explain the reasons for this divergence.

SSA in the Cold War Appears to Have Increased the Incidence of Civil Wars

The differences between the Cold War and post–Cold War eras are also important in terms of impact. There were relatively few consistent relationships between SSA and political violence across African countries. One of the major exceptions was the relationship between SSA and increased incidence of civil wars during the Cold War.

There are at least two explanations for this relationship. First, because the United States emphasized international alignment over domestic stability as the primary goal of its assistance policies, it might have implemented SSA in ways that exacerbated conflict. As our first-stage models suggest, the United States was perfectly willing to collaborate with authoritarian and corrupt governments so long as they were not allies of the Soviet Union. Doing so might have prompted backlash among populations that were excluded from government. Second, the Soviet Union countered U.S. assistance by providing aid to armed opposition movements, touching off proxy wars.

---

[1] See the literature review in Chapter Two of Stephen Watts, *Identifying and Mitigating Risks in Security Sector Assistance for Africa's Fragile States*, Santa Monica, Calif.: RAND Corporation, RR-808-A, 2015.

It is possible, of course, that the relationship between U.S.-provided SSA and civil wars during the Cold War is one of correlation but not causation. In particular, the United States might have steered SSA to partners that were most at risk of insurgency, in which case the risk of insurgency would have been driving SSA allocation rather than the reverse. Although such factors might have contributed to the relationship, we think that it is unlikely to be the primary driver. First, our use of propensity weights was designed to limit the potential bias caused by selection effects. Such a procedure is far from perfect, and selection certainly could have played a role. But we would expect such effects to at least be attenuated by our propensity-weighting procedures. Second, it is not the case that the United States was systematically sending SSA to the most at-risk countries during the Cold War. In fact, according to two of the most-important risk indicators—time since the last civil war and time since the last coup—the United States appeared to be steering clear of some of the most at-risk countries during the Cold War. Instead, it focused on fragile postconflict states in the post–Cold War era. Consequently, it seems likely that SSA did, in fact, contribute to the incidence of civil wars during the Cold War.

This finding is important not just for historical reasons. If international competition for influence in Africa again intensifies, the United States could again be tempted to deemphasize governance issues when it allocates SSA. Our analyses suggest that such an approach risks provoking higher levels of conflict on the continent.

Most SSA in Most Countries in the Post–Cold War Era Appears to Have Had Little Net Impact on Political Violence

We identified no robust relationships between SSA as a whole and political violence across Africa in the post–Cold War era. As we discussed in Chapter Five, the absence of an overall relationship between U.S.-provided SSA and political violence does not necessarily mean that there is no effect. SSA could be having positive and negative effects in different countries at various times, depending on the context, in which case the divergent effects would result in no net impact. Similarly, if some U.S. programs had positive effects and others negative effects, there would be no net result. If the more-expensive forms of

SSA (such as equipment transfers) had no effect while very small-budget programs (such as IMET) or recent programs (such as the SGI) had consistent effects, the much more-expensive programs might obscure the impact of the smaller programs.

We attempted to account for differing contexts and differing SSA programs in a variety of ways. As detailed in Appendix B, we examined SSA's effects conditional on different types of political regimes and other factors in the recipient countries. With one exception (discussed in the next section), these context-specific models provided no more indication than our overall models did of a relationship between SSA and violence. More troubling was our inability to test the effects of specific SSA programs. As discussed in Chapter Two, limitations in the quality and precision of SSA data hindered our ability to test many of the more-nuanced and program-specific relationships that we would have liked to examine. Perhaps particular categories of SSA—especially relatively inexpensive ones and recent ones—are successful. It is equally possible that there are particular categories of SSA that are problematic.[2] Until the U.S. government collects, stores, and disseminates more-precise data on SSA, it will be extremely difficult to conduct reliable statistical tests of more-nuanced and program-specific relationships.

Despite these data limitations, the lack of an aggregate effect of SSA is important. Whatever "success stories" might exist are relatively modest in their impact on political violence, obscured by much larger amounts of inefficient spending, or offset by counterproductive outcomes in other cases. Otherwise, our analyses should have detected some relationship between SSA and the incidence of political violence.

The finding that U.S.-provided SSA has not had any net impact on political violence in the post–Cold War era should not be altogether surprising. Numerous studies have found that African partner nations have failed to sustain much of the equipment the United States has pro-

---

[2] Indeed, the hypothesis that different types of SSA have different effects is central to Savage and Caverley's work on coups (Savage and Caverley, 2017), discussed in Appendix C. Unfortunately, as we discuss in detail in that appendix, we believe that SSA data limitations also hinder the identification of a robust relationship between SSA and coup attempts.

vided.[3] Others have pointed out that many African partner states lack the training infrastructure necessary for "train-the-trainer approaches," so U.S. training activities are often one-off events.[4] Whether because of systemic maintenance problems, lack of training infrastructure, or other causes, the gains the United States' partners realize from SSA are often short-lived. Even if African partners could sustain these gains, they often appear to have difficulties harnessing these capabilities to effective political–military strategies. In some cases, U.S. partners might divert these capabilities to corrupt ends, while, in other cases, they might use them to try to repress nonstate actors where cooptation might be the more stabilizing strategy.[5]

The finding that U.S. assistance in the post–Cold War era has not had any identifiable net effect is an important one. It suggests at a minimum that the United States' efforts are inefficient and wasteful, at least in pursuit of violence reduction. But the fact that there might be more-nuanced, context-specific effects that our analysis missed is also important. If certain types of U.S. SSA are having divergent effects depending on context, it is essential that the United States better employ risk analysis to identify contexts in which SSA is having counterproductive effects. And if much of U.S. SSA is indeed helping to build short-term, tactical capabilities but these capabilities are not sustained or harnessed to an effective political–military strategy, this gap suggests that the United States needs to reallocate SSA to specific programs that it has strong reason to believe will produce outcomes superior to the aggregate effects of SSA.

---

3 See, for instance, McNerney, Johnson, et al., 2016, p. 67.

4 Daniel Hampton, "Creating Sustainable Peacekeeping Capability in Africa," Africa Center for Strategic Studies, Africa Security Brief 27, April 30, 2014.

5 Alice Hills, "Trojan Horses? USAID, Counterterrorism and Africa's Police," *Third World Quarterly*, Vol. 27, No. 4, 2006, pp. 629–643; Robert G. Berschinski, *AFRICOM's Dilemma: The "Global War on Terrorism," "Capacity Building," Humanitarianism, and the Future of U.S. Security Policy in Africa*, Carlisle Barracks, Pa.: Strategic Studies Institute, U.S. Army War College, November 2007, pp. 30–31; Gutelius, 2007, pp. 59–76.

SSA Has Had Significant, Positive Impact in Peacekeeping Contexts

Although SSA has not had any identifiable net effect in most countries on the continent, it has had a significant impact when conducted in conjunction with UN PKOs. Even when controlling for the direct effects of "blue helmets," SSA executed in the presence of peacekeepers has statistically significant, favorable effects on the likelihood of renewed conflict, the likelihood of terrorist attacks, and the likelihood of government repression.

A statistical analysis such as this one cannot uncover the precise reasons for these favorable effects. The findings are entirely consistent with the SSR literature, however. The SSR paradigm emphasizes that the capabilities of security forces should be built in conjunction with improvements to security governance. The presence of a UN PKO typically provides many of the prerequisites necessary for such an approach to succeed: regular, intensive contact between international advisers and the partner nation's security personnel; a relatively long-term commitment; close oversight of the performance of security forces; and the integration of train-and-equip efforts into an overall political strategy. Several of the countries underlying our statistical results—including Burundi, Liberia, and Sierra Leone—are ones that have been held out as success stories of SSR efforts. One of the criticisms of the SSR paradigm has been the relatively thin base of rigorous empirical support for its prescriptions.[6] The statistical results presented in this report lend credence to the SSR prescriptions.

Our results for the effects of SSA in the presence of PKOs are hardly conclusive. They rely on a relatively small number of observations, particularly for the analysis of civil-war onset. We also cannot rule out that other factors are contributing to this result. In particular, because we lacked good data on other countries' SSA, it is hard for us to disentangle the effects of U.S.-provided SSA from SSA provided by its allies, including the United Kingdom in Sierra Leone and the Netherlands in Burundi. That said, the results do pass some other tests. There

---

[6] Ursula C. Schroeder and Fairlie Chappuis, "New Perspectives on Security Sector Reform: The Role of Local Agency and Domestic Politics," *International Peacekeeping*, Vol. 21, No. 2, 2014, pp. 133–148.

is no evidence that UN PKOs by themselves produce more-favorable results, either in models in which PKOs are considered by themselves (as control variables) or in ones in which we included an interaction term with SSA. Moreover, we observed favorable results for the effects of SSA in conjunction with PKOs across nearly all of our outcomes of interest—civil wars, terrorism, and state repression. Certainly, this is a finding that deserves additional research to test the robustness of our results. The initial findings, however, are highly encouraging.

Recommendations for the Allocation and Implementation of SSA

Our results have important implications for how the United States should allocate and implement SSA in the future.

Balance Goals of Achieving Access and Influence with Governance Concerns

In Africa, the United States' primary goals for SSA include BPC to combat irregular threats (such as terrorism) and gaining access to and influence with important partner nations.[7] The record of the Cold War suggests that these two goals can be at odds with one another. In attempting to ensure that partners in Africa remained aligned with the United States rather than the Soviets, the United States might well have aggravated domestic political tensions and ultimately increased the incidence of civil wars on the continent. Looking forward, many observers anticipate increased international competition for influence in Africa. China is the United States' primary concern, but other nations—including Russia, Turkey, and the Gulf states—also play roles. The United States could again be tempted to relegate governance issues to second-tier status in an effort to remain the "security partner

---

[7] A primary goal of SC activities (such as joint exercises) is also to train U.S. military personnel to operate in different environments, such as those in Africa.

of choice."[8] Doing so, however, could come at a sizable cost if it again enflames domestic political rivalries. The United States should balance its efforts to maintain influence in Africa with efforts to build partners' capabilities in a responsible, constructive manner.

Adopt a Comprehensive Approach with Persistent Presence and Oversight

The fact that U.S.-provided SSA had consistently positive effects when implemented in conjunction with UN PKOs suggests that the manner in which SSA is implemented is critical. Much of the SSA that the United States provides is highly episodic, built around particular targets of opportunity. In some cases, planners have had to expend so much effort to cobble together the necessary authorities, programs, and funding that they have had insufficient time remaining to think about how individual SSA efforts fit into a comprehensive political–military approach. Moreover, legislative requirements and shifting senior-level attention often means that efforts cannot be sustained over multiple years. The result is a highly inefficient expenditure of SSA funds, with many or most initiatives demonstrating little enduring impact. This is the conclusion that emerges from our statistical analysis, but it is also the conclusion that many U.S. military personnel have reached through difficult personal experience.[9]

The SSR paradigm suggests that tactical capability-building should be embedded within a comprehensive approach that is appropriate to the local political context, involve close collaboration between international advisers and local stakeholders, and be part of a long-term process. UN PKOs typically provide the organizational "scaffolding" for such an approach. They usually include a sizable number of inter-

---

[8] The Defense Strategic Guidance issued by the Obama administration stated that the United States would seek to be the "security partner of choice" in Africa. See DoD, *Sustaining U.S. Global Leadership: Priorities for 21st Century Defense*, Washington, D.C., Defense Strategic Guidance, January 2012, p. 3. Note that the first-stage models presented in Chapter Five suggest that partner governance has remained a concern in the United States' allocation of SSA even in the post-9/11 era.

[9] See Powelson, 2013, for a particularly insightful firsthand account of many of these issues.

national specialists attuned to local political dynamics and who are located in-country, often over extended periods of time. Indeed, PKOs have provided one of the few contexts in which SSR has succeeded in the past. It is therefore not surprising that we find that U.S.-provided SSA has the greatest positive impact in these environments.

The United States has interests in Africa outside of countries that are hosting PKOs. It consequently needs a model of SSA that works outside of these most-favorable contexts. A handful of U.S. programs—most notably, the SGI—adopt the principles of SSR but attempt to implement them in countries that are not hosting blue helmets. Unfortunately, these programs are of such recent origin that we could not test their effects in our models. The consistently favorable results of SSA in peacekeeping contexts and the absence of impact elsewhere, however, suggest that the United States should continue to find ways to implement these principles elsewhere when feasible.

Conduct Risk Assessments

As discussed in Chapter Five, the fact that SSA has had no net effect in post–Cold War Africa (outside of PKOs) does not mean that there is no effect at all. SSA could be having divergent effects depending on the type of SSA and the context in which it is implemented. We attempted to assess this potential variability by examining the effects of SSA conditional on certain observable characteristics of the implementation environment, such as the economic and political development of the partner nation. As detailed in Appendix B, with the exception of PKOs, we did not find any robust patterns of divergent outcomes. Unfortunately, the SSA data we were able to obtain limited the nuance of the tests we were able to run. One recent study, for instance, found that IMET and CTFP might be related to a higher incidence of coup attempts.[10] In Appendix C, we replicate this study and conduct a deep dive on coups, showing that this finding appears to be highly dependent on how these two programs are measured. To conduct sophisticated tests of these and other programs under different conditions, we

---

[10] Savage and Caverley, 2017.

would need higher-quality data than are currently available over long periods of time and for large numbers of countries.

Nonetheless, the potential for counterproductive effects in certain contexts suggests that U.S. planners should take the concept of political risk seriously. If U.S. planners could successfully anticipate and at least partially mitigate the political risks of SSA through formal risk assessments at the outset of high-risk SSA programs, SSA might start to demonstrate a net positive effect on political violence. Although the statistical evidence of political risk is somewhat ambiguous, many qualitative analyses suggest that this risk should be taken seriously. Some existing frameworks—such as USAID's Conflict Assessment Framework, intended for use globally, and its District Stability Framework, created for use in Afghanistan—provide elements of a risk-assessment framework, but these or similar tools would need to be adapted and further developed for SSA.[11]

Recommendations for Future Assessment, Monitoring, and Evaluation

Although the broad trends identified in this report represent an important baseline for understanding the impact of SSA in Africa, much work remains to be done. Improving monitoring and data collection and dissemination for U.S. SSA is an important first step. There are also numerous opportunities to conduct much more-precise evaluations of SSA's impact in specific countries—evaluations that could help to establish the differential effects of various types of SSA or the myriad ways in which context shapes outcomes. We conclude this report with three suggestions for improved M&E in the future.

Commit to Rigorous Monitoring and Evaluation

The U.S. government has made considerable improvements in the past couple of years in its M&E policies for SSA in Africa and more gen-

---

[11] For a summary of evidence of political risk and the need for political risk assessments, see S. Watts, 2015.

erally. DoD, for instance, recently issued a formal instruction requiring improved M&E for SSA.[12] The Bureau of African Affairs at the State Department has undertaken a sizable and well-conceived effort to conduct extensive performance evaluations of SSA in Africa, with the expectation that these efforts will facilitate rigorous impact evaluations in future years. AFRICOM has launched the Integrated AFRICOM Theater Synchronization System, a software platform for linking individual programs to strategic goals, with links permitting "drill down" into funding information and evaluations. All of these initiatives—and many others—are welcome steps toward systematic evaluations of SSA's effectiveness, but much more remains to be done.

A robust M&E program can yield substantial returns on investment—but only if funding and effort are sustained over time. The U.S. government should continue its efforts to improve program monitoring, systematize data collection and dissemination, and use these inputs for improved evaluations.

Improve the Quality of SSA Data

This report has frequently noted limitations in the data available for SSA evaluations. In many cases, Greenbook data on SSA, for instance, do not correspond to the appropriate country or year. These data are structured by accounting, rather than analytic, requirements, making it difficult to disaggregate accounts into particular types of aid (such as training and advising versus materiel transfers) that might yield different results. But data issues are much more pervasive than simply limitations in the Greenbook figures. Outside of the recent initiatives in the State Department's Bureau of African Affairs, it is often very difficult to determine whether a program was implemented in the way it was intended. And many types of SSA—in particular, SC, such as joint

---

[12] Office of the Under Secretary of Defense for Policy, *Assessment, Monitoring, and Evaluation Policy for the Security Cooperation Enterprise*, Washington, D.C., Department of Defense Instruction 5132.14, January 13, 2017.

exercises—are recorded (if at all) using different systems entirely, many of which are highly incomplete.[13]

There are numerous efforts that the U.S. government might undertake to improve the quality of data available. These range from improved accounting standards to improved guidance on how to write rigorous and useful after-action reports from SC events. Improved data collection is only part of the challenge, however. For data to truly be useful, the U.S. government must also commit to improved knowledge-management practices, including appropriate storage and dissemination.

Conduct In-Depth Evaluations of High-Impact, High-Risk Programs

As efforts to evaluate the effectiveness of development assistance have demonstrated, analyzing the impact of highly complex interventions in foreign countries is a challenging undertaking. No one form of evaluation can hope to grapple with this complexity. Up to this point, most evaluations of SSA have been qualitative, consisting of after-action reports, lessons-learned exercises, academic case studies, and the like. These analyses have provided many useful insights, but they are inherently limited in their ability to delineate broad trends. This study was perhaps the most in-depth quantitative analysis to date of SSA effectiveness in Africa. Although it has shed light on some critically important trends, it still represents only an initial effort.

Improved data collection would permit more-refined cross-national quantitative analyses such as this one. But ideally, such studies would be complemented by narrower, more-focused evaluations with much stronger methods for identifying the precise causal pathway linking international interventions (such as SSA) with the outcomes

---

[13] For overviews of SSA program monitoring and data challenges in DoD, see, for instance, Jefferson P. Marquis, Michael J. McNerney, S. Rebecca Zimmerman, Merrie Archer, Jeremy Boback, and David Stebbins, *Developing an Assessment, Monitoring, and Evaluation Framework for U.S. Department of Defense Security Cooperation*, Santa Monica, Calif.: RAND Corporation, RR-1611-OSD, 2016, and Beth Grill, Michael J. McNerney, Jeremy Boback, Renanah Miles, Cynthia Clapp-Wincek, and David E. Thaler, *Follow the Money: Promoting Greater Transparency in Department of Defense Security Cooperation Reporting*, Santa Monica, Calif.: RAND Corporation, RR-2039-OSD, 2017.

of interest. Randomized-control trials have come to be considered the "gold standard" for project evaluation in the development community. Although such evaluations are much more difficult to conduct in the security sector, some have already been conducted. The Indian state of Rajasthan, for instance, collaborated with researchers at the Massachusetts Institute of Technology to evaluate various reforms for local police departments.[14] Similar evaluations might be undertaken with willing U.S. partners. Even where randomized-control trials are not possible, natural experiments and other rigorous methods of evaluation might be feasible. Such in-depth, rigorous evaluations cannot be used widely, but they could be conducted for experimental or high-risk forms of SSA to help improve the overall state of understanding of the field.

Rigorous evaluations of SSA still remain a nascent enterprise. This report represents a step forward in our understanding of SSA's effects, but much work remains to be done.

---

[14] Abhijit Banerjee, Raghabendra Chattopadhyay, Esther Duflo, Daniel Keniston, and Nina Singh, *Improving Police Performance in Rajasthan, India: Experimental Evidence on Incentives, Managerial Autonomy and Training*, Cambridge, Mass.: National Bureau of Economic Research, Working Paper 17912, revised November 2014.

Bibliography

Africa Center for Strategic Studies, "History," undated. As of September 2, 2017: https://africacenter.org/about/history/

AFRICOM—*See* U.S. Africa Command.

Aksoy, Deniz, David B. Carter, and Joseph Wright, "Terrorism in Dictatorships," *Journal of Politics*, Vol. 74, No. 3, July 2012, pp. 810–826.

Allansson, Marie, Erik Melander, and Lotta Themnér, "Organized Violence, 1989–2016," *Journal of Peace Research*, Vol. 54, No. 4, 2017, pp. 574–587.

Aning, Emmanuel K., "African Crisis Response Initiative and the New African Security (Dis)order," *African Journal of Political Science*, Vol. 6, No. 1, 2001, pp. 43–67.

Arieff, Alexis, *Burundi's Electoral Crisis: In Brief*, Washington, D.C.: Congressional Research Service, R44018, May 14, 2015. As of April 1, 2018: https://fas.org/sgp/crs/row/R44018.pdf

Arlinghaus, Bruce E., *Military Development in Africa: The Political and Economic Risks of Arms Transfers*, Boulder, Colo.: Westview Press, 1984.

Atkinson, Carol, "Does Soft Power Matter? A Comparative Analysis of Student Exchange Programs 1980–2006," *Foreign Policy Analysis*, Vol. 6, No. 1, January 2010, pp. 1–22.

Bachmann, Jan, and Jana Hönke, "'Peace and Security' as Counterterrorism? The Political Effects of Liberal Interventions in Kenya," *African Affairs*, Vol. 109, No. 434, January 1, 2010, pp. 97–114.

Baker, Aryn, "Corruption in Military Defense Spending Could Be Behind Rise in Africa Terror Attacks," *Time*, January 19, 2016. As of April 3, 2018: http://time.com/4184472/military-corruption-africa-terror-attacks/

Banerjee, Abhijit, Raghabendra Chattopadhyay, Esther Duflo, Daniel Keniston, and Nina Singh, *Improving Police Performance in Rajasthan, India: Experimental Evidence on Incentives, Managerial Autonomy and Training*, Cambridge, Mass.: National Bureau of Economic Research, Working Paper 17912, revised November 2014. As of April 3, 2018:
http://www.nber.org/papers/w17912

Bapat, Navin A., "Transnational Terrorism, US Military Aid, and the Incentive to Misrepresent," *Journal of Peace Research*, Vol. 48, No. 3, 2011, pp. 308–318.

Bapat, Navin A., and Sean Zeigler, "Terrorism, Dynamic Commitment Problems, and Military Conflict," *American Journal of Political Science*, Vol. 60, No. 2, April 2016, pp. 337–351.

Bearce, David H., and Daniel C. Tirone, "Foreign Aid Effectiveness and the Strategic Goals of Donor Governments," *Journal of Politics*, Vol. 72, No. 3, July 2010, pp. 837–851.

Beck, Nathaniel, and Jonathan N. Katz, "Modeling Dynamics in Time-Series–Cross-Section Political Economy Data," *Annual Review of Political Science*, Vol. 14, June 2011, pp. 331–352.

Beck, Nathaniel, Jonathan N. Katz, and Richard Tucker, "Taking Time Seriously: Time-Series–Cross-Section Analysis with a Binary Dependent Variable," *American Journal of Political Science*, Vol. 42, No. 4, October 1998, pp. 1260–1288.

Bell, Curtis, and Jun Koga Sudduth, "The Causes and Outcomes of Coup During Civil War," *Journal of Conflict Resolution*, Vol. 61, No. 7, 2017, pp. 1432–1455.

Bell, Sam R., K. Chad Clay, and Carla Martinez Machain, "The Effect of US Troop Deployments on Human Rights," *Journal of Conflict Resolution*, Vol. 61, No. 10, 2017, pp. 2020–2042.

Berschinski, Robert G., *AFRICOM's Dilemma: The "Global War on Terrorism," "Capacity Building," Humanitarianism, and the Future of U.S. Security Policy in Africa*, Carlisle Barracks, Pa.: Strategic Studies Institute, U.S. Army War College, November 2007. As of April 3, 2018:
http://www.dtic.mil/docs/citations/ADA474526

Blanchard, Lauren Ploch, *Statement of Lauren Ploch Blanchard, Specialist in African Affairs, Congressional Research Service, Before the Senate Foreign Relations Committee Subcommittee on Africa and Global Health, Hearing: U.S. Security Assistance in Africa*, Washington, D.C.: Congressional Research Service, June 4, 2015. As of April 3, 2018:
https://www.foreign.senate.gov/imo/media/doc/060415_Blanchard_Testimony.pdf

Blanton, Shannon Lindsey, "Promoting Human Rights and Democracy in the Developing World: U.S. Rhetoric Versus U.S. Arms Exports," *American Journal of Political Science*, Vol. 44, No. 1, January 2000, pp. 123–131.

———, "Foreign Policy in Transition? Human Rights, Democracy, and U.S. Arms Exports," *International Studies Quarterly*, Vol. 49, No. 4, December 2005, pp. 647–667.

Boix, Carles, Michael Miller, and Sebastian Rosato, "A Complete Data Set of Political Regimes, 1800–2007," *Comparative Political Studies*, Vol. 46, No. 12, 2013, pp. 1523–1554.

Bolt, Jutta, and Jan Luiten van Zanden, "The Maddison Project: Collaborative Research on Historical National Accounts," *Economic History Review*, Vol. 67, No. 3, August 2014, pp. 627–651.

Boutton, Andrew, "Of Terrorism and Revenue: Why Foreign Aid Exacerbates Terrorism in Personalist Regimes," *Conflict Management and Peace Science*, December 21, 2016.

Boutton, Andrew, and David B. Carter, "Fair-Weather Allies? Terrorism and the Allocation of US Foreign Aid," *Journal of Conflict Resolution*, Vol. 58, No. 7, 2014, pp. 1144–1173.

Braithwaite, Alex, "Resisting Infection: How State Capacity Conditions Conflict Contagion," *Journal of Peace Research*, Vol. 47, No. 3, 2010, pp. 311–319.

Bräutigam, Deborah A., and Stephen Knack, "Foreign Aid, Institutions, and Governance in Sub-Saharan Africa," *Economic Development and Cultural Change*, Vol. 52, No. 2, January 2004, pp. 255–285.

Buhaug, Halvard, Lars-Erik Cederman, and Kristian Skrede Gleditsch, "Square Pegs in Round Holes: Inequalities, Grievances, and Civil War," *International Studies Quarterly*, Vol. 58, No. 2, June 2014, pp. 418–431.

Buhaug, Halvard, Lars-Erik Cederman, and Jan Ketil Rød, "Disaggregating Ethno-Nationalist Civil Wars: A Dyadic Test of Exclusion Theory," *International Organization*, Vol. 62, No. 3, Summer 2008, pp. 531–551.

Buhaug, Halvard, and Kristian Skrede Gleditsch, "Contagion or Confusion? Why Conflicts Cluster in Space," *International Studies Quarterly*, Vol. 52, No. 2, June 2008, pp. 215–233.

Burbidge, John G., Lonnie Magee, and A. Leslie Robb, "Alternative Transformations to Handle Extreme Values of the Dependent Variable," *Journal of the American Statistical Association*, Vol. 83, No. 401, March 1988, pp. 123–127.

"Burkina Faso Military Installs General as New Head of State After Coup," *Guardian*, September 17, 2015. As of June 1, 2018:
https://www.theguardian.com/world/2015/sep/18/burkina-faso-military-installs-general-as-new-head-of-state-after-coup

"Burkina Faso's Lt Col Isaac Zida Named Prime Minister," *BBC*, November 19, 2014. As of April 3, 2018:
http://www.bbc.com/news/world-africa-30113675

Bush, George W., *The National Security Strategy of the United States of America*, Washington, D.C.: Executive Office of the President, September 2002. As of April 3, 2018:
https://georgewbush-whitehouse.archives.gov/nsc/nss/2002/

Carter, David B., and Curtis S. Signorino, "Back to the Future: Modeling Time Dependence in Binary Data," *Political Analysis*, Vol. 18, No. 3, Summer 2010, pp. 271–292.

Cederman, Lars-Erik, Nils B. Weidmann, and Kristian Skrede Gleditsch, "Horizontal Inequalities and Ethnonationalist Civil War: A Global Comparison," *American Political Science Review*, Vol. 105, No. 3, August 2011, pp. 478–495.

Cederman, Lars-Erik, Andreas Wimmer, and Brian Min, "Why Do Ethnic Groups Rebel? New Data and Analysis," *World Politics*, Vol. 62, No. 1, January 2010, pp. 87–119.

Center for Systemic Peace, "Polity IV Annual Time-Series, 1800–2016," undated. As of April 3, 2018:
http://www.systemicpeace.org/inscrdata.html

Cingranelli, David L., David L. Richards, and K. Chad Clay, "The CIRI Human Rights Dataset," CIRI Human Rights Data Project, version 2014.04.14, April 4, 2014. As of April 3, 2018:
http://www.humanrightsdata.com/p/data-documentation.html

Clapham, Christopher S., *Africa and the International System: The Politics of State Survival*, New York: Cambridge University Press, 1996.

Clark, Mari, Rolf Sartorius, and Michael Bamberger, *Monitoring and Evaluation: Some Tools, Methods and Approaches*, Washington, D.C.: World Bank, working paper, January 9, 2004. As of April 3, 2018:
http://documents.worldbank.org/curated/en/829171468180901329/
Monitoring-and-evaluation-some-tools-methods-and-approaches

Collier, Paul, and Anke Hoeffler, "Greed and Grievance in Civil War," *Oxford Economic Papers*, Vol. 56, 2004, pp. 563–595.

Commander, AFRICOM—*See* Commander, U.S. Africa Command.

Commander, U.S. Africa Command, *Theater Campaign Plan 2000–16*, August 18, 2015, not available to the general public.

"Congressional Control of Foreign Assistance to Post-Coup States: Assessing Executive Compliance from Honduras to Egypt," *Harvard Law Review*, Vol. 127, No. 8, June 20, 2014, pp. 2499–2520. As of April 3, 2018:
https://harvardlawreview.org/2014/06/
congressional-control-of-foreign-assistance-to-post-coup-states/

Cooper, Helene, "Rifts Between U.S. and Nigeria Impeding Fight Against Boko Haram," *New York Times*, January 24, 2015. As of April 3, 2018: https://www.nytimes.com/2015/01/25/world/rifts-between-us-and-nigeria-impeding-fight-against-boko-haram.html

Cooperative Biological Engagement Program, Cooperative Threat Reduction Program, U.S. Department of Defense, *FY 2015 Annual Accomplishments*, Washington, D.C., September 16, 2016. As of September 30, 2017: http://www.dtra.mil/Portals/61/Documents/Missions/CBEP%20FY15%20Annual%20Accomplishments.pdf?ver=2016-09-16-150152-690

Cunningham, David E., Kristian Skrede Gleditsch, and Idean Salehyan, "It Takes Two: A Dyadic Analysis of Civil War Duration and Outcome," *Journal of Conflict Resolution*, Vol. 53, No. 4, August 2009, pp. 570–597.

Danneman, Nathan, and Emily Hencken Ritter, "Contagious Rebellion and Preemptive Repression," *Journal of Conflict Resolution*, Vol. 58, No. 2, 2014, pp. 254–279.

Defense Security Cooperation Agency, "International Military Education and Training (IMET)," undated (a). As of September 2, 2017: http://www.dsca.mil/programs/international-military-education-training-imet

———, "SAMM Chapters," undated (b). As of September 5, 2017: http://www.samm.dsca.mil/listing/chapters

———, *Security Cooperation Programs, Fiscal Year 2016*, Washington, D.C., revision 16, c. 2016. As of September 2, 2017: http://www.disam.dsca.mil/documents/pubs/security_cooperation_programs_160127.pdf

Dietrich, John W., "U.S. Human Rights Policy in the Post–Cold War Era," *Political Science Quarterly*, Vol. 121, No. 2, Summer 2006, pp. 269–294.

DoD—*See* U.S. Department of Defense.

DoD and U.S. Department of State—*See* U.S. Department of Defense and U.S. Department of State.

DSCA—*See* Defense Security Cooperation Agency.

Dube, Oeindrila, and Suresh Naidu, "Bases, Bullets, and Ballots: The Effect of US Military Aid on Political Conflict in Colombia," *Journal of Politics*, Vol. 77, No. 1, January 2015, pp. 249–267.

Enders, Walter, Todd Sandler, and Khusrav Gaibulloev, "Domestic Versus Transnational Terrorism: Data, Decomposition, and Dynamics," *Journal of Peace Research*, Vol. 48, No. 3, 2011, pp. 319–337.

Farah, Douglas, "U.S. to Help Nigeria Revamp Its Armed Forces," *Washington Post*, April 29, 2000. As of April 3, 2018:
https://www.washingtonpost.com/archive/politics/2000/04/29/us-to-help-nigeria-revamp-its-armed-forces/eab2413a-3264-4812-8375-ca1c54fa6d29/

Fearon, James D., and David D. Laitin, "Ethnicity, Insurgency, and Civil War," *American Political Science Review*, Vol. 97, No. 1, February 2003, pp. 75–90.

Felter, Joseph H., *Taking Guns to a Knife Fight: Effective Military Support to COIN*, Carlisle Barracks, Pa.: U.S. Army War College, Senior Service College fellowship project, January 4, 2009.

Findley, Michael J., and Joseph K. Young, "Terrorism and Civil War: A Spatial and Temporal Approach to a Conceptual Problem," *Perspectives on Politics*, Vol. 10, No. 2, June 2012a, pp. 285–305.

———, "More Combatant Groups, More Terror? Empirical Tests of an Outbidding Logic," *Terrorism and Political Violence*, Vol. 24, No. 5, November 2012b, pp. 706–721.

Finley, J. C., "White House Weighs In on Situation in Burkina Faso," UPI, October 30, 2014. As of April 3, 2018:
https://www.upi.com/Top_News/World-News/2014/10/30/White-House-weighs-in-on-situation-in-Burkina-Faso/8961414685647/

Fitch, John Samuel, "The Political Impact of U.S. Military Aid to Latin America," *Armed Forces and Society*, Vol. 5, No. 3, 1979, pp. 360–386.

———, "Human Rights and the U.S. Military Training Program: Alternatives for Latin America," *Human Rights Quarterly*, Vol. 3, No. 4, November 1981, pp. 65–80.

Fjelde, Hanne, "Generals, Dictators, and Kings: Authoritarian Regimes and Civil Conflict, 1973–2004," *Conflict Management and Peace Science*, Vol. 27, No. 3, 2010, pp. 185–218.

Florquin, Nicolas, and Jonah Leff, "Across Conflict Zones: Ammunition Profiling," in *Small Arms Survey 2014: Women and Guns*, Geneva: Small Arms Survey, 2014, pp. 178–211. As of April 3, 2018:
http://www.smallarmssurvey.org/publications/by-type/yearbook/small-arms-survey-2014.html

Fortna, Virginia Page, "Do Terrorists Win? Rebels' Use of Terrorism and Civil War Outcomes," *International Organization*, Vol. 69, No. 3, Summer 2015, pp. 519–556.

Framework for Peace in the Middle East and Framework for the Conclusion of a Peace Treaty Between Egypt and Israel, Israel–Egypt–United States, September 17, 1978. As of June 12, 2018:
https://peacemaker.un.org/egyptisrael-frameworkforpeace78

Gartzke, Erik, *The Affinity of Nations Index, 1946–2002*, version 4.0, New York: Columbia University, March 10, 2006.

Gift, Thomas, and Daniel Krcmaric, "Who Democratizes? Western-Educated Leaders and Regime Transitions," *Journal of Conflict Resolution*, Vol. 61, No. 3, 2017, pp. 671–701.

Gleditsch, Kristian Skrede, "Transnational Dimensions of Civil War," *Journal of Peace Research*, Vol. 44, No. 3, 2007, pp. 293–309.

Gleditsch, Nils Petter, Peter Wallensteen, Mikael Eriksson, Margareta Sollenberg, and Håvard Strand, "Armed Conflict 1946–2001: A New Dataset," *Journal of Peace Research*, Vol. 39, No. 5, 2002, pp. 615–637.

Grill, Beth, Michael J. McNerney, Jeremy Boback, Renanah Miles, Cynthia Clapp-Wincek, and David E. Thaler, *Follow the Money: Promoting Greater Transparency in Department of Defense Security Cooperation Reporting*, Santa Monica, Calif.: RAND Corporation, RR-2039-OSD, 2017. As of April 3, 2018: https://www.rand.org/pubs/research_reports/RR2039.html

Grimmett, Richard F., *International Military Education and Training Program*, Washington, D.C.: Congressional Research Service, RS20506, October 28, 2004. As of April 3, 2018:
https://www.hsdl.org/?view&did=717523

Gutelius, David, "Islam in Northern Mali and the War on Terror," *Journal of Contemporary African Studies*, Vol. 25, No. 1, 2007, pp. 59–76.

Haber, Stephen, and Victor Menaldo, "Do Natural Resources Fuel Authoritarianism? A Reappraisal of the Resource Curse," *American Political Science Review*, Vol. 105, No. 1, February 2011, pp. 1–26.

Hampton, Daniel, "Creating Sustainable Peacekeeping Capability in Africa," Africa Center for Strategic Studies, Africa Security Brief 27, April 30, 2014. As of April 3, 2018:
https://africacenter.org/publication/creating-sustainable-peacekeeping-capability-in-africa/

Hanauer, Larry, and Stephanie Pezard, *Security Cooperation Amidst Political Uncertainty: An Agenda for Future Research*, Santa Monica, Calif.: RAND Corporation, WR-1052, 2014. As of April 3, 2018:
https://www.rand.org/pubs/working_papers/WR1052.html

Harkness, Kristen A., "The Ethnic Army and the State: Explaining Coup Traps and the Difficulties of Democratization in Africa," *Journal of Conflict Resolution*, Vol. 60, No. 4, 2016, pp. 587–616.

Hartung, William D., "Military Aid Should Do No Harm: The Failures of U.S. Military Assistance Programs Far Outpace the Successes," *U.S. News and World Report*, March 8, 2016. As of September 20, 2017:
https://www.usnews.com/opinion/blogs/world-report/articles/2016-03-08/us-military-aid-does-too-much-harm

Heckman, James J., *Sample Selection Bias as a Specification Error (with an Application to the Estimation of Labor Supply Functions)*, Cambridge, Mass.: National Bureau of Economic Research, Working Paper 172, March 1977. As of May 29, 2018:
http://www.nber.org/papers/w0172

Hegre, Håvard, Tanja Ellingsen, Scott Gates, and Nils Petter Gleditsch, "Toward a Democratic Civil Peace? Democracy, Political Change, and Civil War, 1816–1992," *American Political Science Review*, Vol. 95, No. 1, March 2001, pp. 33–48.

Hendrix, Cullen S., and Joseph K. Young, "State Capacity and Terrorism: A Two-Dimensional Approach," *Security Studies*, Vol. 23, No. 2, 2014, pp. 329–363.

Herskovits, Jean, professor of history, State University of New York, *The Nigerian Transition and the Future of U.S. Policy*, testimony before the U.S. Senate Committee on Foreign Relations, 106th Congress, 1st session, November 4, 1999. As of September 20, 2017:
https://www.gpo.gov/fdsys/pkg/CHRG-106shrg61867/html/CHRG-106shrg61867.htm

Hills, Alice, "Trojan Horses? USAID, Counterterrorism and Africa's Police," *Third World Quarterly*, Vol. 27, No. 4, 2006, pp. 629–643.

Honaker, James, and Gary King, "What to Do About Missing Values in Time-Series Cross-Section Data," *American Journal of Political Science*, Vol. 54, No. 2, April 2010, pp. 561–581.

International Institute for Strategic Studies, *The Military Balance*, Vol. 114, No. 1, 2014.

Jackson, Rose, *Untangling the Web: A Blueprint for Reforming American Security Sector Assistance*, Washington, D.C.: Open Society Foundations, January 2017. As of April 3, 2018:
https://www.opensocietyfoundations.org/reports/untangling-web-blueprint-reforming-american-security-sector-assistance

Jones, Seth G., Andrew Liepman, and Nathan Chandler, *Counterterrorism and Counterinsurgency in Somalia: Assessing the Campaign Against al Shabaab*, Santa Monica, Calif.: RAND Corporation, RR-1539-OSD, 2016. As of April 3, 2018:
https://www.rand.org/pubs/research_reports/RR1539.html

Jones, Seth G., Olga Oliker, Peter Chalk, C. Christine Fair, Rollie Lal, and James Dobbins, *Securing Tyrants or Fostering Reform? U.S. Internal Security Assistance to Repressive and Transitioning Regimes*, Santa Monica, Calif.: RAND Corporation, MG-550-OSI, 2006. As of April 3, 2018:
https://www.rand.org/pubs/monographs/MG550.html

Jourde, Cédric, "The International Relations of Small Neoauthoritarian States: Islamism, Warlordism, and the Framing of Stability," *International Studies Quarterly*, Vol. 51, No. 2, June 2007, pp. 481–503.

Karim, Sabrina M., and William A. Wagstaff, "Keeping the Peace After Peacekeeping: How Peacekeepers Resolve the Security Dilemma in Post-Conflict States," unpublished paper.

Keele, Luke, and Nathan J. Kelly, "Dynamic Models for Dynamic Theories: The Ins and Outs of Lagged Dependent Variables," *Political Analysis*, Vol. 14, No. 2, Spring 2006, pp. 186–205.

Keshi, Joe, "America–Nigeria Troubled Relations," *Vanguard*, October 24, 2014. As of September 20, 2017:
https://www.vanguardngr.com/2014/10/america-nigeria-troubled-relations/

Kleinfeld, Rachel, *Fragility and Security Sector Reform*, Washington, D.C.: U.S. Institute of Peace, September 27, 2016. As of April 3, 2018:
https://www.usip.org/publications/2016/09/fragility-and-security-sector-reform

Kugler, Jacek, and Ronald L. Tammen, eds., *The Performance of Nations*, Lanham, Md.: Rowman and Littlefield, 2012.

LaFree, Gary, Laura Dugan, and Erin Miller, *Putting Terrorism in Context: Lessons from the Global Terrorism Database*, Abingdon, Oxon: Routledge, 2015.

Lai, Brian, and Daniel S. Morey, "Impact of Regime Type on the Influence of U.S. Foreign Aid," *Foreign Policy Analysis*, Vol. 2, No. 4, October 2006, pp. 385–404.

Lamb, Robert D., Kathryn Mixon, and Andrew Halterman, *Absorptive Capacity in the Security and Justice Sectors: Assessing Obstacles to Success in the Donor–Recipient Relationship*, Washington, D.C.: Center for Strategic and International Studies, June 28, 2013. As of April 3, 2018:
https://www.csis.org/analysis/absorptive-capacity-security-and-justice-sectors

Lawson, Letitia, "External Democracy Promotion in Africa: Another False Start?" *Commonwealth and Comparative Politics*, Vol. 37, No. 1, 1999, pp. 1–30.

———, "U.S. Africa Policy Since the Cold War," *Strategic Insights*, Vol. 6, No. 1, January 2007. As of April 3, 2018:
http://www.dtic.mil/get-tr-doc/pdf?AD=ADA520352

Leon, Gabriel, "Loyalty for Sale? Military Spending and Coups d'État," *Public Choice*, Vol. 159, Nos. 3–4, June 2014, pp. 363–383.

Lloyd, Alec, "U.S. Air Forces Africa Help Nigerian C-130 Fly Again," U.S. Africa Command, September 1, 2009. As of April 3, 2018:
http://www.africom.mil/media-room/article/6845/us-air-forces-africa-help-nigerian-c-130-fly-again

Londregan, John B., and Keith T. Poole, "Poverty, the Coup Trap, and the Seizure of Executive Power," *World Politics*, Vol. 42, No. 2, January 1990, pp. 151–183.

Lujala, Päivi, "Deadly Combat over Natural Resources: Gems, Petroleum, Drugs, and the Severity of Armed Civil Conflict," *Journal of Conflict Resolution*, Vol. 53, No. 1, 2009, pp. 50–71.

———, "The Spoils of Nature: Armed Civil Conflict and Rebel Access to Natural Resources," *Journal of Peace Research*, Vol. 47, No. 1, 2010, pp. 15–28.

"Mali Crisis: US Admits Mistakes in Training Local Troops," *BBC*, January 25, 2013. As of April 3, 2018:
http://www.bbc.com/news/world-africa-21195371

Marinov, Nikolay, and Hein Goemans, "Coups and Democracy," *British Journal of Political Science*, Vol. 44, No. 4, October 2014, pp. 799–825.

Marquis, Jefferson P., Michael J. McNerney, S. Rebecca Zimmerman, Merrie Archer, Jeremy Boback, and David Stebbins, *Developing an Assessment, Monitoring, and Evaluation Framework for U.S. Department of Defense Security Cooperation*, Santa Monica, Calif.: RAND Corporation, RR-1611-OSD, 2016. As of April 3, 2018:
https://www.rand.org/pubs/research_reports/RR1611.html

Masaki, Takaaki, "*Coups d'État* and Foreign Aid," *World Development*, Vol. 79, March 2016, pp. 51–68.

McCormick, Ty, "Is the U.S. Military Propping Up Uganda's 'Elected' Autocrat?" *Foreign Policy*, February 18, 2016. As of April 3, 2018:
http://foreignpolicy.com/2016/02/18/is-the-us-military-propping-up-ugandas-elected-autocrat-museveni-elections/

McFate, Sean, *Building Better Armies: An Insider's Account of Liberia*, Carlisle Barracks, Pa.: U.S. Army War College, Strategic Studies Institute, November 2013. As of April 3, 2018:
https://ssi.armywarcollege.edu/pubs/display.cfm?pubID=1181

McKinney, Edward, "Don't Bend the Law to Fight Terror in Nigeria," *National Interest*, June 2, 2016. As of April 6, 2018:
http://nationalinterest.org/feature/dont-bend-the-law-fight-terror-nigeria-16440

McNerney, Michael J., Jonah Blank, Becca Wasser, Jeremy Boback, and Alexander Stephenson, *Improving Implementation of the Department of Defense Leahy Law*, Santa Monica, Calif.: RAND Corporation, RR-1737-OSD, 2017. As of April 3, 2018:
https://www.rand.org/pubs/research_reports/RR1737.html

McNerney, Michael J., Stuart E. Johnson, Stephanie Pezard, David Stebbins, Renanah Miles, Angela O'Mahony, Chaoling Feng, and Tim Oliver, *Defense Institution Building in Africa: An Assessment*, Santa Monica, Calif.: RAND Corporation, RR-1232-OSD, 2016. As of April 3, 2018:
https://www.rand.org/pubs/research_reports/RR1232.html

McNerney, Michael J., Angela O'Mahony, Thomas S. Szayna, Derek Eaton, Caroline Baxter, Colin P. Clarke, Emma Cutrufello, Michael McGee, Heather Peterson, Leslie Adrienne Payne, and Calin Trenkov-Wermuth, *Assessing Security Cooperation as a Preventive Tool*, Santa Monica, Calif.: RAND Corporation, RR-350-A, 2014. As of April 3, 2018:
https://www.rand.org/pubs/research_reports/RR350.html

Meernik, James, Eric L. Krueger, and Steven C. Poe, "Testing Models of U.S. Foreign Policy: Foreign Aid During and After the Cold War," *Journal of Politics*, Vol. 60, No. 1, February 1998, pp. 63–85.

Metz, Steven, *Reform, Conflict, and Security in Zaire*, Carlisle Barracks, Pa.: U.S. Army War College, Strategic Studies Institute, June 5, 1996. As of April 3, 2018:
https://ssi.armywarcollege.edu/pubs/display.cfm?pubID=203

Mitchell, Neil J., Sabine C. Carey, and Christopher K. Butler, "The Impact of Pro-Government Militias on Human Rights Violations," *International Interactions*, Vol. 40, No. 5, 2014, pp. 812–836.

Moyar, Mark, *Aid for Elites: Building Partner Nations and Ending Poverty Through Human Capital*, New York: Cambridge University Press, 2016.

Muller, Edward N., "Income Inequality, Regime Repressiveness, and Political Violence," *American Sociological Review*, Vol. 50, No. 1, February 1985, pp. 47–61.

Mutual Security Agency, *Mutual Defense Assistance Control Act of 1951: Public Law 213—82d Congress: First Report to Congress*, Vols. 1–8, Washington, D.C., October 15, 1952.

National Consortium for the Study of Terrorism and Responses to Terrorism, "Global Terrorism Database," last updated June 2017. As of 2016:
https://www.start.umd.edu/gtd

Nossiter, Adam, Eric Schmitt, and Mark Mazzetti, "French Strikes in Mali Supplant Caution of U.S.," *New York Times*, January 13, 2013. As of April 3, 2018:
https://www.nytimes.com/2013/01/14/world/africa/french-jets-strike-deep-inside-islamist-held-mali.html

OECD—*See* Organisation for Economic Co-operation and Development.

Office of the Assistant Secretary of Defense for Special Operations and Low Intensity Conflict, *Regional Defense Combating Terrorism Fellowship Program: Report to Congress, Fiscal Year 2015*, Washington, D.C.: U.S. Department of Defense, c. 2015. As of April 3, 2018:
https://www.hsdl.org/?abstract&did=794761

Office of the Under Secretary of Defense (Comptroller), *Fiscal Year (FY) 2018 President's Budget: Justification for FY 2018 Operation and Maintenance, Defense-Wide*, Washington, D.C.: U.S. Department of Defense, May 2017. As of April 3, 2018:
http://comptroller.defense.gov/Budget-Materials/FY2018BudgetJustification/

Office of the Under Secretary of Defense for Policy, *Assessment, Monitoring, and Evaluation Policy for the Security Cooperation Enterprise*, Washington, D.C., Department of Defense Instruction 5132.14, January 13, 2017. As of April 3, 2018:
http://open.defense.gov/portals/23/Documents/foreignasst/DoDI_513214_on_AM&E.pdf

Organisation for Economic Co-operation and Development, "Net ODA," undated. As of June 1, 2018:
https://data.oecd.org/oda/net-oda.htm

———, *The OECD DAC Handbook on Security System Reform: Supporting Security and Justice*, Paris: Organisation for Economic Co-operation and Development, Development Assistance Committee, February 25, 2008.

Passage, David, *The United States and Colombia: Untying the Gordian Knot*, Carlisle, Pa.: Strategic Studies Institute, U.S. Army War College, March 2000. As of April 6, 2018:
http://ssi.armywarcollege.edu/pdffiles/00027.pdf

Paul, Christopher, Colin P. Clarke, Beth Grill, Stephanie Young, Jennifer D. P. Moroney, Joe Hogler, and Christine Leah, *What Works Best When Building Partner Capacity and Under What Circumstances?* Santa Monica, Calif.: RAND Corporation, MG-1253/1-OSD, 2013. As of April 3, 2018:
https://www.rand.org/pubs/monographs/MG1253z1.html

Paul, Christopher, Michael Nixon, Heather Peterson, Beth Grill, and Jessica Yeats, *The RAND Security Cooperation Prioritization and Propensity Matching Tool*, Santa Monica, Calif.: RAND Corporation, TL-112-OSD, 2013. As of April 3, 2018:
https://www.rand.org/pubs/tools/TL112.html

Piazza, James A., "Incubators of Terror: Do Failed and Failing States Promote Transnational Terrorism?" *International Studies Quarterly*, Vol. 52, No. 3, September 2008, pp. 469–488.

Pilster, Ulrich, and Tobias Böhmelt, "Coup-Proofing and Military Effectiveness in Interstate Wars, 1967–1999," *Conflict Management and Peace Science*, Vol. 28, No. 4, 2011, pp. 331–350.

Poe, Steven C., and James Meernik, "US Military Aid in the 1980s: A Global Analysis," *Journal of Peace Research*, Vol. 32, No. 4, 1995, pp. 399–411.

Posen, Barry R., "The Security Dilemma and Ethnic Conflict," *Survival*, Vol. 35, No. 1, Spring 1993, pp. 27–47.

Powell, Jonathan M., "Determinants of the Attempting and Outcome of Coups d'État," *Journal of Conflict Resolution*, Vol. 56, No. 6, 2012, pp. 1017–1040.

———, "Trading Coups for Civil War: The Strategic Logic of Tolerating Rebellion," *African Security Review*, Vol. 23, No. 4, 2014, pp. 328–338.

Powell, Jonathan M., and Clayton L. Thyne, "Global Instances of Coups from 1950 to 2010: A New Dataset," *Journal of Peace Research*, Vol. 48, No. 2, 2011, pp. 249–259.

Powelson, Simon J., *Enduring Engagement Yes, Episodic Engagement No: Lessons for SOF from Mali*, Monterey, Calif.: Naval Postgraduate School, master's thesis, December 2013. As of April 3, 2018:
https://calhoun.nps.edu/handle/10945/38996

Public Law 87-195, Foreign Assistance Act of 1961, September 4, 1961.

Public Law 93-559, Foreign Assistance Act of 1974, December 30, 1974.

Public Law 108-375, Ronald W. Reagan National Defense Authorization Act for Fiscal Year 2005, October 28, 2004. As of April 6, 2018:
https://www.gpo.gov/fdsys/pkg/PLAW-108publ375/content-detail.html

Public Law 112-74, Consolidated Appropriations Act, 2012, Section 7043(d), Expanded International Military Education and Training, December 23, 2011. As of April 3, 2018:
https://www.gpo.gov/fdsys/pkg/PLAW-112publ74/content-detail.html

Public Law 114-328, National Defense Authorization Act for Fiscal Year 2017, December 23, 2016. As of April 5, 2018:
https://www.gpo.gov/fdsys/pkg/PLAW-114publ328/content-detail.html

Ritter, Emily Hencken, "Policy Disputes, Political Survival, and the Onset and Severity of State Repression," *Journal of Conflict Resolution*, Vol. 58, No. 1, 2014, pp. 143–168.

Rodrik, Dani, "The New Development Economics: We Shall Experiment, but How Shall We Learn?" in Jessica Cohen and William Easterly, eds., *What Works in Development? Thinking Big and Thinking Small*, Washington, D.C.: Brookings Institution Press, November 3, 2009, pp. 24–47.

Roessler, Philip, "The Enemy Within: Personal Rule, Coups, and Civil War in Africa," *World Politics*, Vol. 63, No. 2, April 2011, pp. 300–346.

Ross, Thomas W., "Defining the Discipline in Theory and Practice," in Alexandra Kerr and Michael Miklaucic, eds., *Effective, Legitimate, Secure: Insights for Defense Institution Building*, Washington, D.C.: Center for Complex Operations, Institute for National Strategic Studies, National Defense University, 2017, pp. 21–46. As of May 29, 2018:
https://purl.fdlp.gov/GPO/gpo86964

Ruby, Tomislav Z., and Douglas Gibler, "US Professional Military Education and Democratization Abroad," *European Journal of International Relations*, Vol. 16, No. 3, 2010, pp. 339–364.

Savage, Jesse Dillon, and Jonathan D. Caverley, "When Human Capital Threatens the Capitol: Foreign Aid in the Form of Military Training and Coups," *Journal of Peace Research*, Vol. 54, No. 4, 2017, pp. 542–557.

Schmitt, Eric, "U.S. Training Elite Antiterror Troops in Four African Nations," *New York Times*, May 26, 2014. As of April 3, 2018:
https://www.nytimes.com/2014/05/27/world/africa/us-trains-african-commandos-to-fight-terrorism.html

Schnabel, Albrecht, "Ideal Requirements Versus Real Environments in Security Sector Reform," in Hans Born and Albrecht Schnabel, eds., *Security Sector Reform in Challenging Environments*, Geneva: Geneva Centre for the Democratic Control of Armed Forces, 2009, pp. 3–38. As of April 3, 2018:
https://www.dcaf.ch/security-sector-reform-challenging-environments

Schroeder, Ursula C., and Fairlie Chappuis, "New Perspectives on Security Sector Reform: The Role of Local Agency and Domestic Politics," *International Peacekeeping*, Vol. 21, No. 2, 2014, pp. 133–148.

Sen, Ashish Kumar, "Nigerian President Slams US Law," Atlantic Council, July 22, 2015.

Serafino, Nina M., *Department of Defense "Section 1207" Security and Stabilization Assistance: Background and Congressional Concerns, FY2006–FY2010*, Washington, D.C.: Congressional Research Service, RS22871, March 3, 2011. As of April 3, 2018:
https://www.hsdl.org/?abstract&did=741130

———, *Security Assistance and Cooperation: Shared Responsibility of the Departments of State and Defense*, Washington, D.C.: Congressional Research Service, R44444, April 4, 2016. As of April 3, 2018:
http://www.dtic.mil/docs/citations/AD1013554

Serafino, Nina M., June S. Beittel, Lauren Ploch Blanchard, and Liana Rosen, *"Leahy Law" Human Rights Provisions and Security Assistance: Issue Overview*, Washington, D.C.: Congressional Research Service, R43361, January 29, 2014. As of April 3, 2018:
https://www.hsdl.org/?abstract&did=749254

Singer, J. David, "Reconstructing the Correlates of War Dataset on Material Capabilities of States, 1816–1985," *International Interactions*, Vol. 14, No. 2, 1988, pp. 115–132.

Skorupski, Bolko J., and Nina M. Serafino, *DoD Security Cooperation: An Overview of Authorities and Issues*, Washington, D.C.: Congressional Research Service, R44602, August 23, 2016. As of April 3, 2018:
http://www.dtic.mil/docs/citations/AD1015381

Stewart, Phil, "U.S. Commander Seeks to Ease Human-Rights Rules That Limit Training," Reuters, March 6, 2013. As of April 3, 2018: https://www.reuters.com/article/us-usa-military-rights/u-s-commander-seeks-to-ease-human-rights-rules-that-limit-training-idUSBRE9251NB20130306

Stoker, Donald, "The Evolution of Foreign Military Advising and Assistance, 1815–2005," in Kendall D. Gott and Michael G. Brooks, eds., *Security Assistance: U.S. and International Historical Perspectives—The Proceedings of the Combat Studies Institute 2006 Military History Symposium*, Fort Leavenworth, Kan.: Combat Studies Institute Press, 2006, pp. 33–44. As of April 3, 2018: https://usacac.army.mil/sites/default/files/documents/cace/CSI/CSIPubs/2006Symposium.pdf

Sullivan, Patricia L., Brock F. Tessman, and Xiaojun Li, "US Military Aid and Recipient State Cooperation," *Foreign Policy Analysis*, Vol. 7, No. 3, July 2011, pp. 275–294.

Temin, Jon, "Somalia and the Limits of U.S. Bombing," *New York Times*, May 25, 2017. As of April 3, 2018: https://www.nytimes.com/2017/05/25/opinion/somalia-al-shabaab-us-airstrikes.html

Thyne, Clayton, "The Impact of Coups d'État on Civil War Duration," *Conflict Management and Peace Science*, Vol. 34, No. 3, 2017, pp. 287–307.

Tierney, Michael J., Daniel L. Nielson, Darren G. Hawkins, J. Timmons Roberts, Michael G. Findley, Ryan M. Powers, Bradley Parks, Sven E. Wilson, and Robert L. Hicks, "More Dollars Than Sense: Refining Our Knowledge of Development Finance Using AidData," *World Development*, Vol. 39, No. 11, November 2011, pp. 1891–1906.

Toft, Monica Duffy, *Securing the Peace: The Durable Settlement of Civil Wars*, Princeton, N.J.: Princeton University Press, 2010.

Turse, Nick, "Even AFRICOM's Own Commander Admits Its Strategy Is Not Working," *Nation*, August 2, 2016. As of August 13, 2017: https://www.thenation.com/article/even-africoms-own-commander-admits-their-strategy-is-not-working/

———, "Can the Pentagon Win When Putsch Comes to Shove? A Rare Pentagon 'Success' Story," *Salon*, August 11, 2017. As of September 20, 2017: http://www.salon.com/2017/08/11/can-the-pentagon-win-when-putsch-comes-to-shove_partner/

UN General Assembly Security Council—*See* United Nations General Assembly Security Council.

UN Security Council—*See* United Nations Security Council.

United Nations General Assembly Security Council, *Report of the Panel on United Nations Peace Operations* (commonly known as the Brahimi Report), A/55/305–S/2000/809, August 1, 2000. As of April 3, 2018:
https://reliefweb.int/report/world/report-panel-united-nations-peace-operations-a55305-s2000809

United Nations Security Council, *Special Report of the Secretary-General on the United Nations Mission in Liberia*, S/2016/968, November 15, 2016. As of April 3, 2018:
https://reliefweb.int/report/liberia/special-report-secretary-general-united-nations-mission-liberia-s2016968

———, "Despite Progress Since Peace Accord, Mali Still Needs International Support to Face Accelerating Challenges, Peacekeeping Chief Tells Security Council," 7,917th meeting, SC/12779, April 6, 2017. As of September 25, 2017:
https://www.un.org/press/en/2017/sc12779.doc.htm

Urdal, Henrik, "A Clash of Generations? Youth Bulges and Political Violence," *International Studies Quarterly*, Vol. 50, No. 3, September 2006, pp. 607–629.

U.S. Africa Command, "Exercises," undated (a). As of September 2, 2017:
http://www.africom.mil/what-we-do/exercises

———, "National Guard State Partnership Program," undated (b). As of September 2, 2017:
http://www.africom.mil/what-we-do/security-cooperation/national-guard-state-partnership-program

U.S. Agency for International Development, *Assessing and Learning: ADS Chapter 203*, Washington, D.C., partial revision, February 10, 2012. As of April 3, 2018:
http://usaidprojectstarter.org/sites/default/files/resources/pdfs/203.pdf

———, *U.S. Overseas Loans and Grants: Obligations and Loan Authorizations, July 1, 1945–September 30, 2016*, CONG-R-0105, c. 2016. As of April 3, 2018:
https://explorer.usaid.gov/reports.html#greenbook

USAID—*See* U.S. Agency for International Development.

U.S. Code, Title 10, Armed Forces, Subtitle A, General Military Law, Part IV, Service, Supply, and Procurement, Chapter 136, Provisions Relating to Specific Programs, Section 2282, Authority to Build the Capacity of Foreign Security Forces. As of April 5, 2018:
https://www.gpo.gov/fdsys/granule/USCODE-2014-title10/USCODE-2014-title10-subtitleA-partIV-chap136-sec2282/content-detail.html

U.S. Code, Title 32, National Guard. As of June 12, 2018:
https://www.govinfo.gov/app/details/USCODE-2016-title32/

U.S. Department of Defense, *Sustaining U.S. Global Leadership: Priorities for 21st Century Defense*, Washington, D.C., Defense Strategic Guidance, January 2012. As of April 3, 2018:
http://nssarchive.us/national-defense-strategy/defense_strategic_guidance/

U.S. Department of Defense and U.S. Department of State, *Foreign Military Training: Fiscal Years 2014 and 2015—Joint Report to Congress: Volume I*, Washington, D.C., c. 2015. As of April 3, 2018:
https://www.state.gov/documents/organization/243009.pdf

U.S. Department of State, "Global Security Contingency Fund (GSCF)," undated (a). As of September 25, 2017:
https://www.state.gov/t/pm/gpi/gscf/index.htm

———, Office of the Historian, "The Angola Crisis: 1974–75," undated (b). As of September 17, 2017:
https://history.state.gov/milestones/1969-1976/angola

———, Office of the Historian, "The Congo, Decolonization, and the Cold War: 1960–1965," undated (c). As of September 17, 2017:
https://history.state.gov/milestones/1961-1968/congo-decolonization

———, Office of the Coordinator for Counterterrorism, *Country Reports on Terrorism 2007*, Washington, D.C., April 2008. As of September 17, 2017:
https://www.state.gov/documents/organization/105904.pdf

———, Bureau of African Affairs, *Security Governance Initiative: 2015 Review*, Washington, D.C., March 2, 2016a. As of April 3, 2018:
https://2009-2017.state.gov/p/af/rls/2016/253906.htm

———, Bureau of Counterterrorism and Countering Violent Extremism, "Country Reports: Africa Overview," in *Country Reports on Terrorism 2015*, Washington, D.C., June 2, 2016b. As of September 20, 2017:
https://www.state.gov/j/ct/rls/crt/2015/257514.htm

U.S. Government Accountability Office, *Combating Terrorism: State Department Can Improve Management of East Africa Program*, Washington, D.C., GAO-14-502, June 17, 2014a. As of April 3, 2018:
https://www.gao.gov/products/GAO-14-502

———, *Combating Terrorism: U.S. Efforts in Northwest Africa Would Be Strengthened by Enhanced Program Management*, Washington, D.C., GAO-14-518, June 24, 2014b. As of April 3, 2018:
https://www.gao.gov/products/GAO-14-518

Vines, Lisa, "AFRICOM and National Guard Leaders Meet to Discuss State Partnership Program," U.S. Africa Command, February 2, 2016. As of October 2, 2017:
https://www.africom.mil/media-room/article/27927/
africom-and-national-guard-leaders-meet-to-discuss-state-partnership-program

Waldhauser, Thomas D., *General Thomas D. Waldhauser, Commander, U.S. Africa Command: Prepared Opening Statement, U.S. Senate Armed Services Committee, March 9, 2017*, statement before the U.S. Senate Committee on Armed Services, March 9, 2017a. As of August 13, 2017:
http://www.africom.mil/media-room/document/28722/africom-commander-prepared-opening-comments-to-sasc

———, *United States Africa Command 2017 Posture Statement*, statement before the U.S. Senate Committee on Armed Services, March 9, 2017b. As of April 5, 2018:
http://www.africom.mil/media-room/document/28720/africom-2017-posture-satement

Walter, Barbara F., "Does Conflict Beget Conflict? Explaining Recurring Civil War," *Journal of Peace Research*, Vol. 41, No. 3, 2004, pp. 371–388.

Wang, T. Y., "Arms Transfers and Coups d'État: A Study on Sub-Saharan Africa," *Journal of Peace Research*, Vol. 35, No. 6, 1998, pp. 659–675.

Watts, Clint, Jacob Shapiro, and Vahid Brown, *Al-Qa'ida's (Mis)Adventures in the Horn of Africa*, West Point, N.Y.: Combating Terrorism Center at West Point, July 2, 2007. As of April 3, 2018:
https://ctc.usma.edu/al-qaidas-misadventures-in-the-horn-of-africa/

Watts, Stephen, *Identifying and Mitigating Risks in Security Sector Assistance for Africa's Fragile States*, Santa Monica, Calif.: RAND Corporation, RR-808-A, 2015. As of April 3, 2018:
https://www.rand.org/pubs/research_reports/RR808.html

Weiss, Caleb, "Shabaab Releases Photos from Captured African Union Base," *Threat Matrix*, January 21, 2016. As of January 6, 2018:
https://www.longwarjournal.org/archives/2016/01/shabaab-releases-photos-from-captured-african-union-base.php

Whitaker, Beth Elise, "Reluctant Partners: Fighting Terrorism and Promoting Democracy in Kenya," *International Studies Perspectives*, Vol. 9, No. 3, August 2008, pp. 254–271.

White House, Office of the Press Secretary, "Fact Sheet: U.S. Security Sector Assistance Policy," Presidential Policy Directive 23, April 5, 2013. As of April 5, 2018:
https://www.hsdl.org/?abstract&did=747214

Whitlock, Craig, "Coup Leader in Burkina Faso Received U.S. Military Training," *Washington Post*, November 3, 2014. As of April 3, 2018:
https://www.washingtonpost.com/world/national-security/coup-leader-in-burkina-faso-received-us-military-training/2014/11/03/3e9acaf8-6392-11e4-836c-83bc4f26eb67_story.html

Williams, Paul D., with Abdirashid Hashi, *Exit Strategy Challenges for the AU Mission in Somalia*, Mogadishu, Somalia: Heritage Institute for Policy Studies, February 2016. As of April 3, 2018:
http://www.heritageinstitute.org/exit-strategy-challenges-for-the-au-mission-in-somalia/

Wilson, Matthew C., and James A. Piazza, "Autocracies and Terrorism: Conditioning Effects of Authoritarian Regime Type on Terrorist Attacks," *American Journal of Political Science*, Vol. 57, No. 4, October 2013, pp. 941–955.

Wimmer, Andreas, Lars-Erik Cederman, and Brian Min, "Ethnic Politics and Armed Conflict: A Configurational Analysis of a New Global Data Set," *American Sociological Review*, Vol. 74, No. 2, 2009, pp. 316–337.

World Bank, *World Development Indicators 2012*, Washington, D.C., 2012. As of April 3, 2018:
https://openknowledge.worldbank.org/handle/10986/6014

Wright, Joseph, Erica Frantz, and Barbara Geddes, "Oil and Autocratic Regime Survival," *British Journal of Political Science*, Vol. 45, No. 2, April 2015, pp. 287–306.